A WORD GEOGRAPHY
OF CALIFORNIA AND NEVADA

BY

ELIZABETH S. BRIGHT

UNIVERSITY OF CALIFORNIA PRESS
BERKELEY · LOS ANGELES · LONDON
1971

UNIVERSITY OF CALIFORNIA PUBLICATIONS IN LINGUISTICS

Advisory Editors: W. E. Bull, W. L. Chafe, M. B. Emeneau, M. R. Haas,
Harry Hoijer, L. D. Newmark, D. L. Olmsted, W. F. Shipley, R. P. Stockwell

Volume 69

Approved for publication April 14, 1970
Issued December 22, 1971

University of California Press
Berkeley and Los Angeles
California

University of California Press, Ltd.
London, England

ISBN: 0-520-09367
Library of Congress Catalog Card No.: 79-631460-4
© 1971 by The Regents of the University of California

CONTENTS

Preface   ix

I.   What Is a Word Geography?   1

II. Geographical and Historical Summary   4

III. Analysis of the California-Nevada Vocabulary 40

IV. The Relation of California-Nevada Vocabulary to
     the Speech of Other Regions 118

V.   Summary 137

Appendix:
     The California-Nevada Vocabulary 139
     A Selected Bibliography 209

Index of Terms 211

MAPS

1. Locations of Missions, Presidios, and Pueblos 9
2. The California Trail 12
3. The Old Spanish and Santa Fe Trails 13
4. Salt Lake to Los Angeles. 13
5. The Gila Trail and Butterfield Stage Route 14

California Population Maps

6. Population percentage 1870 24
7. Population percentage 1880 25
8. Population percentage from New York 1870 26
9. Population percentage from Missouri 1870 27
10. Population percentage from Ohio 1870 28
11. Population percentage from Maine 1870 29
12. Population percentage from Massachusetts 1870 30
13. Population percentage from Illinois 1880 31
14. Population percentage from Pennsylvania 1880 32

Nevada Population Maps

15. Population percentage 1870 and 1880 34
16. Population percentage from New York 1870 35
17. Population percentage from California 1870 36
18. Population percentage from Ohio 1870 37
19. Population percentage from Illinois 1870 38
20. Population percentage from Utah 1880 39

21. Linguistic Atlas of the Pacific Coast Communities 44
22. Geographic Areas for Distribution Study 45

Isogloss Maps

California:

23. Isogloss I 49
24. Isogloss II 51
25. Isogloss III 53
26. Isogloss IV 55
27. Isogloss V 57
28. Isogloss VI 59
29. Pattern VI percentage of usage 61
30. Isogloss VII 62
31. Isogloss VIII 64
32. Isogloss IX 67
33. Isogloss X 68
34. Isogloss XI 70
35. Isogloss XII 72
36. Isogloss XIIIa 77
37. Isogloss XIIIb 78
38. Isogloss XIIIc 79
39. Isogloss XIV 81
40. Isogloss XVa 83
41. Isogloss XVb 84

Nevada:

42. Isogloss XVI 91
43. Isogloss XVIIa 92
44. Isogloss XVIIb 93
45. Isogloss XVIII 95
46. Isogloss XIX 97

47. Pattern XX Composite of I-XV 99
48. Occurrence of Spanish Borrowings 101
49. Occurrence of Thirteen Most Common Spanish Words 104
50. Rodéo/ródeo 105
51. Occurrences of Borrowings other than Spanish 109

TABLES

1. Explanation of Map 1 8
2. Approximate Dates of Modern Settlement of Communities used in the Linguistic Atlas of the Pacific Coast 18
3. Population Characteristics: Graphs 22
4. Communities of the Linguistic Atlas of the Pacific Coast. . . . 42

Isogloss Lists and Distribution Density Charts:
5. Pattern I. 48
6. Pattern II 50
7. Pattern III 52
8. Pattern IV 54
9. Pattern V 56
10. Pattern VI 60
11. Pattern VII 63
12. Pattern VIII 65
13. Pattern IX 66
14. Pattern X 69
15. Pattern XI 71
16. Pattern XII 73
17. Pattern XIIIa, b, c 75
18. Pattern XIV 80
19. Pattern XV 82
20. Comparison of Distribution, California and Nevada 86
21. Pattern XVI 87
22. Pattern XVIIa 88
23. Pattern XVIIb 89
24. Pattern XVIII 94
25. Pattern XIX 96
26. Pattern XX Composite Percentages 100
27. Spanish Borrowings 102
28. Americanizations 103
29. Comparisons of Tables 27 and 28 by Percentages 106
30. Distribution of Thirteen Most Common Spanish Words 107
31. Borrowings other than Spanish 110
32. Folk Terms 113

Comparisons with Other Atlases:
33. Terms in Common with East and Others 123
34. Terms in Common with Regions other than East 128
35. California-Nevada Variants 134

PREFACE

The systematic study of regional differences in American speech was initiated by Hans Kurath, whose Linguistic Atlas of New England was published in 1939. Professor Kurath's work has formed the basis of similar studies in various sections of the country, the ultimate goal being, of course, an atlas of the entire United States.

A word geography is concerned with only one aspect of a linguistic atlas—vocabulary. In addition to Professor Kurath's Word Geography of the Eastern United States (1949), there have been detailed studies of Texas, the Great Lakes region, and Colorado, as well as several minor reports of other areas. The general purpose of such a study is to show in what ways and to what extent the language is affected by the geography and history of a region by analyzing the reflection of these influences that is discernible in the vocabulary of those who have lived most of their lives in the area under study.

Because of the unique character of the California-Nevada background, both geographically and historically, I have departed somewhat from the form of other word geographies in presenting the general vocabulary that has evolved from the mingling of speech forms brought from all parts of the United States by the migrants—words that have outlasted the competition generally—as well as those terms that have survived only regionally or locally. Items that were used in other studies but occurred in only one or two responses in this area were not included. In other words, it seems more important, for example, that kerosene and coal oil are both used by a large percentage of California-Nevada informants distributed generally over the two states than that the term lamp oil has survived with four individuals as widely scattered as Sacramento and Las Vegas.

This work was first undertaken as a doctoral dissertation under the direction of Professor David W. Reed at the University of California, Berkeley. I am indebted to him not only for making the field records of the Linguistic Atlas of the Pacific Coast available to me but also for his guidance throughout the work.

To

Maxel Lyle Bright

CHAPTER I

WHAT IS A WORD GEOGRAPHY?

What words we and our neighbors use and how we pronounce them have had an interest for people through the ages. But it has been only since the late nineteenth century that this interest has developed into a scientific study with the aim of understanding the forces that bring about language change through the study of the pronunciation, syntax, and vocabulary of regional speech. The purpose of a word geography is to find the regional distribution of expressions commonly used in the everyday life of people in both urban and rural areas. "It is the vocabulary in this range of life that gives us insight into the structure of speech areas, trade areas, and culture areas, and the trend from local to regional and national usage."[1]

The material on which this study is based is taken from the field records of the Linguistic Atlas of the Pacific Coast, which, under the direction of Professor David W. Reed, were completed in 1959. The three hundred interviews contained in the field records were gathered from informants throughout the two states as follows: Los Angeles, 55; San Francisco, 25; East Bay, 20; San Diego, 8; Peninsula, 5; Sacramento, 5; San Bernardino, 4; Stockton, 3; San Jose, 3; Fresno, 3; Bakersfield, 3; Pomona, 3; Riverside, 3; and 2 each in sixty-seven other California communities and fifteen Nevada communities.

Informants were selected on the basis of certain residence, age, and education requirements. In order to reflect the native stable element of the population, the informant must have spent eighteen of his first twenty years and three-fourths of his entire life in the community.

Age requirements were:

Old	60 and above
Middle-aged	45-60
Young	30-45

[1]Hans Kurath, A Word Geography of the Eastern United States (Ann Arbor, 1949), p. 10.

[1]

Education requirements were:

Uneducated	not past eighth grade
Educated	any amount of high school and technical education such as business college
College group	graduates if possible

In rural communities where only two informants were selected, they were picked from the old/middle-aged, educated/uneducated groups insofar as possible. Similarly, in urban communities 2/5 were in each of these categories and 1/5 in the young and college categories. Consideration was also given to political, religious, and other social affiliations in order to maintain as even a distribution as possible. Information was elicited by trained field workers in personal interviews with the informants.

The questionnaire consisted of 600 items and about 800 questions. The list of items that were known to be divided in usage was compiled from questionnaires of studies that had already been conducted, with that of the eastern United States used as the core and others, such as that used in the Great Lakes region, adapted as needed. In addition, items that were suspected of being regional or local in distribution were incorporated with the others. The categories in which the items may be classified are generally those of everyday family life as well as those of a rural and agricultural nature: time, weather, food, furniture and household goods, buildings and building materials, farm implements and animals, crops, topography, native plants and animals, grammatical forms, pronunciation items, etc. All of the items except those that were included for pronunciation only (e.g., numbers, such as twenty, hundred, the fifth man) have been used in this study. Occasionally pronunciation items produced lexical variants: these, of course, were included in the vocabulary list.

For a number of reasons the California-Nevada region has particular value in the study of the spread of word usage westward across the United States. First, as an area of comparatively recent settlement, California-Nevada can be regarded as a transition area—that is, an area in which the speech characteristics of adjacent regions meet and compete for acceptance.

Second, because of the geographical variety of the region, the effect of natural barriers such as mountains, rivers, deserts, and ocean on the flow of speech can be readily observed.

Third, California-Nevada is a linguistic microcosm in which the processes of linguistic change which normally take place over a long period of time were speeded up by the rapidity of settlement brought about by the Gold Rush, the discovery of the Comstock Lode, the completion of the transcontinental railroad, and the resulting land boom (all of which took place during a period of a little over half a century).

Fourth, California provides an excellent opportunity to study what happens when one language is brought into a region where another language has been in general use. In this case, English was brought in and imposed as the dominant language over Spanish, which had been the prestige language up to that time.

And finally, for the study of word usage in relation to language change to be meaningful, we must be able to discern from the common speech the interaction of geographical and historical forces as it is reflected in the everyday lives and activities of the people. By filling in one of the gaps in the overall pattern of the country, we come one step closer to understanding the factors which have helped to shape American English.

CHAPTER II

GEOGRAPHICAL AND HISTORICAL SUMMARY

GEOGRAPHY

Isolation has been a major factor in determining the rate and areas of settlement of California and Nevada. Even during the Indian period there was little, if any, communication between California Indians and tribes of other parts of the country. The matter of distance, not only from the eastern part of the United States but also from Europe, is one reason the exploration and settlement of this area took place at a much later date than that of most of the rest of the country. Probably more important, however, were the natural barriers, which at first discouraged exploration, especially by land, and later were determining factors in deciding the routes that the migration trails would take.

On the east the entire state of Nevada and the eastern part of California to the Sierra Nevada lie in the Great Basin, which extends from the Rockies to the Sierra. The term "basin" is somewhat misleading, because the region is broken by several short ranges of mountains running usually in a north-south direction. Most of the rivers have no outlet to the sea, but rather end in sinks in the basin, as do, for example, the Humboldt and Carson rivers. The only outlets to the sea are through tributaries of the Snake River and the Colorado River. For the most part it is an extremely arid region, which ends in the south in the Mojave and Colorado deserts.

Rising abruptly from the basin on the west and varying from forty to eighty miles in width, the Sierra Nevada runs north and south for some four hundred miles. The passes over the range, such as Beckwith,[1] Donner, Carson, and Walker passes, have played an important part in the settlement history of the state. North of the Sierra Nevada, the Cascade Range continues north into Oregon, and in the extreme northeast corner of the state is a high, volcanic plateau, the Modoc.

[1]So used by George Stewart in The California Trail (New York, 1962). On some maps and in some books it is referred to as "Beckwourth" and "Beckworth."

[4]

Across the northern end of California, from the Cascades to the Pacific and also continuing north into Oregon, are the Klamath Mountains.

In the heart of the state is the great Central Valley, drained from the north by the Sacramento River and from the south by the San Joaquin River, both of which find a common outlet in San Francisco Bay. The valley is bound on the west by the Coast Ranges, a series of mountains running from the northwest to the southeast which extend south until they meet the Transverse Ranges. The areas of settlement of the Coast Ranges are for the most part in the inland valleys, such as Napa-Livermore, Santa Clara, and Salinas valleys. The mountains fall off rather abruptly into the ocean, leaving at best little more than a narrow shelf along the coast, with the three main bays of Humboldt, San Francisco, and Monterey.

At the southern end of the Coast Ranges, the Transverse Ranges run east and west, and the Tehachapi Mountains on the eastern end join the Sierra Nevada. Thus a natural wall is formed between the northern and southern parts of the state. The Transverse Ranges, together with the Peninsula Ranges, form a semicircle between the coastal plain which extends from the Los Angeles area to San Diego, and the Mojave and Colorado deserts on the east. Again, we find that the passes through these mountains, such as the Tejon between the San Fernando and San Joaquin valleys and the Cajon between the Mojave Desert and San Bernardino, have played an important part in the settlement patterns. Because this area is drier than the northern part, the availability of water has been a deciding factor in the choice of the sites of early settlement, and the valleys of San Bernardino, San Gabriel, and Elsinore were among the first to be settled.

The natural San Diego Bay and the man-made Los Angeles Harbor at San Pedro are the main shipping points of the south coast.

The great variety in land formations leads also to variety in industries: grazing and mining in the arid parts; mining, lumbering, and grazing in the foothills and rugged mountainous areas; farming and ranching in the central and coastal valleys, and also in the valleys of Southern California with the development of irrigation; fishing along the coast; petroleum production in the southern San Joaquin Valley and in Southern California; and shipping from the larger harbors. Until recent years California was mainly an agricultural state; not until the period of World War II did it become important as a manufacturing state.

The history of the migration into this region reflects the restraints imposed on settlement by these geographical characteristics.

HISTORY OF SETTLEMENT

California

The Indian Period

When the Spanish arrived in California, there were about 130,000 Indians inhabiting the area, it has been estimated, with approximately 64,000 of that number affected by the missions. Their basic political unit was the village; therefore it has been more convenient to identify them by language similarities than by tribes. Twenty-one linguistic families have been identified, having 135 regional dialects. These can be further reduced to about half a dozen unrelated groups: Penutian, Hokan, Shoshonean, Yukian, Athabascan, Algonkin, and Lutuamian.[2] They were not a nomadic people, each tribe having well-defined and well-respected boundaries, and conditions for the existence of dialects were excellent. William Bright points out that a number of dialects and languages became extinct without having been adequately recorded, estimating that sixteen languages had perished without adequate study.[3] The Indian languages were submerged under two waves of migration, the Spanish imposing their own language on the natives of the region, just as the Americans imposed English on the Californios later; therefore it is not surprising that for the most part only in place names do we find traces of the Indian languages that were once spoken in this area.

The Spanish Period—1542-1821

The first Spaniard in California was Juan Rodriguez Cabrillo, who sailed into San Diego Bay in 1542. The first settlement was also San Diego, but it was not founded until 1769. This lag between discovery and settlement was the result of several factors: one, the isolated position from Spain and from the Spanish outposts in Mexico; two, the fact that in 1615 Juan de Iturbe had reported Baja California to be an island, a misconception which was not corrected until 1701 by the Kino expedition; three, the concentration of Spanish interests on the search for gold in Mexico and New Mexico.

[2] Information on the Indian population was taken from A. L. Kroeber, *Handbook of the Indians of California*. Bulletin 78 of the Bureau of American Ethnology (Washington, D.C., 1925), pp. 880-891.

[3] William Bright, ed., *Studies in Californian Linguistics*, UCPL, vol. 34 (Berkeley, 1964), p. vii.

The founding of San Diego in 1769 was a joint undertaking of military and missionary forces under the leadership of Don Gaspar de Portolá and Father Junípero Serra respectively. This was the first of the string of missions which was established along El Camino Real, and which eventually extended up the coast as far north as Sonoma. The choice of sites, influenced by the need for water and suitable land for raising crops, resulted in confining the colonization of the new territory to the coastal valleys, and under neither the Spanish nor the Mexican rule was there much penetration of the interior valleys or mountains.

The Spanish settlements were of three types: the missions, which undertook the conversion and education of the Indians; the presidios, military establishments for the protection of the missions and towns; the pueblos, civilian towns established to provide supplies for the military establishments. Insofar as possible the colonies were to be self-supporting (map 1, table 1).

Spain was not the only nation to show an interest in the western part of the continent. Sir Francis Drake, representing England, landed somewhere along the northern California coast (the exact spot is still disputed) as early as 1579. Ships sailing to the Orient soon found they could trade for fur, hides, and tallow along the California coast. Under Spanish rule such trade was forbidden but was carried on illegally by British and American traders, especially New Englanders, who wanted hides for the shoe industry. Russians, seeking seals and sea otters for their fur trade, established Fort Ross north of the Golden Gate in 1812 with 100 Russians and 80 Aleuts. The supply of otters and other fur-bearing animals declined in the Mexican era, and Fort Ross was sold to Captain John Sutter in 1841, and today only the buildings of the old fort remain to remind Californians that Russia once had a foothold on the coast. For the most part, the Spanish discouraged any attempt by other nations to develop interests in the California province, so that it was not until the Mexican rule that Americans could openly trade with Californians.

The Mexican Period—1821-1846

Mexico gained its independence from Spain in 1821 and thus took control over California. The Mexican government immediately started the secularization of the missions. The last mission, Santa Clara, was closed in 1836. The Indian population had already been reduced by the diseases brought in by the white man. With the closing of the missions the condition of the Indians worsened, and with the discovery of gold

Table 1

Explanation of Map 1

1. San Francisco Solano (Sonoma), mission, est. 1823.
2. San Rafael Arcángel, mission, est. 1817.
3. San Francisco de Assisi, mission and presidio, est. 1776.
4. Santa Clara, mission, est. 1777.
5. San José de Guadalupe, mission and pueblo, est. 1797.
6. Branciforte, pueblo, est. 1797.
7. Santa Cruz, mission, est. 1791.
8. San Juan Bautista, mission, est. 1797.
9. San Carlos Borroméo, mission and presidio (Monterey), est. 1770.
10. Nuestra Señora de la Soledad, mission, est. 1791.
11. San Antonio de Padua, mission, est. 1771.
12. San Miguel Arcángel, mission, est. 1797.
13. San Luís Obispo de Tolosa, mission, est. 1772.
14. Purísima Concepción, mission, est. 1787.
15. Santa Inés, mission, est. 1804.
16. Santa Barbara, mission, est. 1786; presidio, est. 1782.
17. San Buenaventura, mission, est. 1782.
18. San Fernando Rey de España, mission, est. 1797.
19. Los Angeles, pueblo, est. 1781.
20. San Gabriel Arcángel, mission, est. 1771.
21. San Juan Capistrano, mission, est. 1776.
22. San Luís Rey de Francia, mission, est. 1798.
23. San Diego de Alcalá, mission and presidio, est. 1769.

San Francisco Solano
San Rafael Arcángel
San Francisco de Asisi
San José de Guadalupe
Santa Clara
Branciforte
Santa Cruz
San Juan Bautista
San Carlos Borroméo
Nuestra Señora de la Soledad
San Antonio de Padua
San Miguel Arcángel
San Luís Obispo de Tolosa
Purísima Concepción
Santa Inés
Santa Barbara
San Fernando Rey de España
San Buenaventura
San Gabriel Arcángel
Los Angeles
San Juan Capistrano
San Luís Rey de Francia
San Diego de Alcalá

LOCATION
of
MISSIONS, PRESIDIOS and PUEBLOS

Map 1

and the influx of miners their food supplies were destroyed and their lands taken from them. Malnutrition and starvation reduced their number to an estimated 16,000 by 1900.[4]

[4] Andrew F. Rolle, California: A History (New York, 1963), p. 29. Also Kroeber, note 2, above.

The lands of the missions were returned to the public domain and were given out by the Mexican government in land grants to private owners. There had been land grants under the Spanish rule, but the owners were usually required to live in the pueblos, and the grants were not as large as those given by the Mexican government. One needed only to be a Mexican of good character or, if a foreigner, to accept Mexican nationality and the Catholic faith, to qualify for eleven square leagues of land.[5] Ranching became almost the only industry in California, and the pastoral life of this period is indeed pleasant to read about.

It was about this time that the American "mountain men"—explorers, trappers, hunters, fur traders—found their way into California. Jedediah Smith was the first to come overland by way of the Old Spanish Trail (map 3) to Los Angeles in 1826, returning up the Central Valley and across the Sierra. Thus the first crossing of the Sierra Nevada by an American was from west to east. Some of these early Americans and Europeans (not only the mountain men, but some of the earlier traders who had come by ship) married natives and remained in the region, or even became Mexican citizens in order to qualify for land grants. As has been noted, the Spanish and Mexicans had settled mainly in the coastal area and had done little to explore or settle the inland valleys: these were the places that the newcomers generally took, Captain Sutter, for instance, in the Sacramento Valley and John Marsh near Mount Diablo.

Even before the discovery of gold, emigrant parties from the states were heading west, looking for new lands on which to settle. The year 1841 marks the beginning of the movement of American settlers to California. In that year the Bidwell-Bartleson party set out from the Missouri in May, traveling by way of South Pass, Bear Valley, across Nevada by the Humboldt and Carson rivers to Walker River, over the Sierra and down the Stanislaus River to the San Joaquin Valley, which they reached in October.

In the same year another party of twenty-five followed the Santa Fe Trail and the Old Spanish Trail (map 3) across southern Utah and Nevada, the Mojave Desert, and over Cajon Pass to Los Angeles.

By 1845 John Marsh estimated the number of Americans in California to be about 700, with 100 English, Scotch and Irish, and an equal number of other Europeans, mainly German, French, and Italian. The Spanish he estimated at 7,000 and domesticated Indians at 10,000.[6]

[5] Rolle, p. 112.
[6] Rolle, p. 186.

The American Period—1846-to Present

Up to this time the penetration of California had been carried on more or less peacefully by traders, trappers, and settlers; many historians think that, had it not been for the Mexican War, the territory would have been annexed peacefully to the United States in due time. As it turned out, however, the declaration of war hastened the process, and in July of 1846 Commodore John D. Sloat took possession at Monterey in the name of the United States. Except for a revolt of Californians around Los Angeles, which was put down by January, 1847, there was little resistance to the change.

It was the discovery of gold at Sutter's mill in 1848 that effected the greatest change in the destiny of the state. It added such impetus to the number of people migrating from the east that by the end of 1849 the population exceeded 100,000; by 1852, 224,325; and in 1860 the official census was 380,015.[7]

Another effect was in the determination of the areas of settlement. San Francisco became the center for providing supplies for the mines and miners, and the outlet for the gold that was mined. Many towns owe their existence to the period of the gold rush, especially the foothill towns such as Auburn, Placerville, and Jackson. Sacramento and Stockton also became places of importance during this time, but differed from the other gold rush towns in adapting to commercial and agricultural industries later, and consequently they maintained their growth even after the rush died down. Northern California in general became the goal of the Forty-niners, and settlement in the southern part suffered accordingly, even though some of the migrants came in by way of the southern route.

There were three main routes by which the pioneers came overland from the east. The northernmost, and the one most used, was the California Trail (map 2). Starting from the Missouri River, it followed the general trail to the west but cut off southwest around Fort Hall or Fort Bridger. It followed the Humboldt River across Nevada and at the foot of the Sierra took one of several routes across the mountains. The northernmost of these, the Lassen route, cut off from the main trail at the big bend of the Humboldt, went northwest across the Black Rock Desert to the northeastern corner of California, then swung down the Pit River and south between the Cascades and the Sierra, and down the Sacramento Valley—a route without the difficult passes that were found farther south but one which was much longer and very difficult in the desert country it had to cross. William H. Nobles later shortened the route considerably by turning west at Black Rock Desert, skirting the Smoke Creek Desert, crossing the mountains easily, and continuing almost due west, north of Mount Lassen, to Shasta City.

[7]John W. Caughey, California, 2nd ed. (Englewood Cliffs, N. J., 1953), p. 256.

THE CALIFORNIA TRAIL

Map 2

Those who continued down the Humboldt River found several passes available to them from the foot of the Sierra Nevada. The Beckwith road turned northwest off the Truckee River, over the Beckwith pass and down the Feather River. Probably the most traveled were the two that crossed near Lake Tahoe—one that followed the Truckee River, crossing the Donner Pass north of Lake Tahoe and proceeding to Auburn; the other following the Carson River and crossing south of Lake Tahoe to Placerville. Even farther south was the road which followed the Walker River and crossed to Sonora. And some chose to follow the Owens River south, cross the Walker Pass, and proceed down the Kern River and north up the San Joaquin Walley.

Another of the main trails was the Old Spanish Trail from Santa Fe to Los Angeles (map 3). It ran northwest from Santa Fe across the southwest corner of Colorado into central Utah, then southwest to the corner of Utah and across the Mojave Desert near present-day Barstow and Victorville and over Cajon Pass to San Bernardino, San Gabriel, and Los Angeles. To go north to the gold fields, the gold hunters would not always go into Los Angeles but would cut across San Fernando Valley and take the Tejon Pass to Bakersfield and proceed up the San Joaquin Valley. The trail from Salt Lake ran south, passing east of Utah Lake, and joined the Old Spanish Trail near Parowan north of Cedar City. This route later became much used as a freight line between Salt Lake City and Los Angeles (map 4)

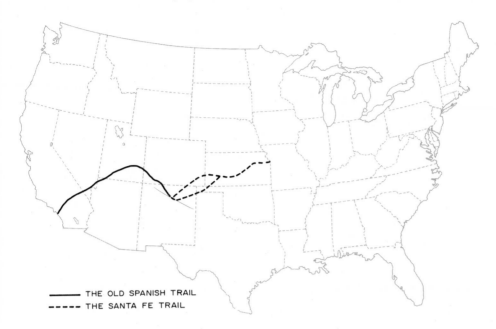

THE OLD SPANISH TRAIL
----- THE SANTA FE TRAIL

Map 3

SALT LAKE to LOS ANGELES

Map 4

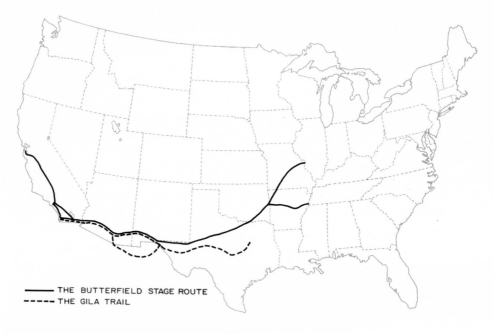

THE BUTTERFIELD STAGE ROUTE
THE GILA TRAIL

Map 5

The southernmost of the routes was the Gila Trail, which had the advantage of being open all year but which proved difficult to traverse because of the scarcity of water. From the heart of Texas it ran west to El Paso, swung south into Mexico, west across Guadalupe Pass and up to Tucson. From there it followed the Gila River to Yuma, crossed the Colorado River into California, and went north by Lake Elsinore to Tejon Pass and so up the valley. An alternate road from El Paso followed the Cooke wagon road by way of Lordsburg to Tucson. At the point where the road turned west, connections were made with a trail which came south from Santa Fe, so that, although the Gila was the southern route, it was possible for immigrants from the midwest to enter California by this trail too. The Gila was also the trail followed by the Butterfield Stage (started 1858). The route, with eastern connections at St. Louis and Memphis, ran to Fort Smith, Arkansas, thence to Sherman, Texas, and across to the Pecos Valley and to El Paso, where it then followed the alternate Gila Trail (map 5).

It has been estimated that approximately 60,000 people entered California by the Gila Trail during the gold rush years.[8] Another estimate of 30,000 over the California Trail in 1849 alone gives some idea of the numbers that must have come overland during these years, although there was no accurate count.[9] However not all of the Forty-niners came overland; from the eastern seaboard many followed the sea route "around the Horn" or to Panama, where they crossed the isthmus and took another

[8]Ralph Moody, The Old Trails West (New York, 1963), p. 93.
[9]Rolle, p. 214.

ship from the Pacific side. Caughey states that "in nine months 549 vessels arrived at San Francisco, many of course from Europe, South America, Mexico, and Hawaii, but about half from the Atlantic seaboard."[10]

The peak year for gold production—$81,294,700—was in 1852. By the middle of the decade the surface had been fairly well cleaned and the individual miner was no longer able to find the "easy money."[11] Thereafter mining was conducted by companies who could raise the capital to buy the machinery needed for such undertakings. Individuals either returned to their homes in the east or turned to other occupations in California, such as farming and ranching. It was not until 1859, with the discovery of the Comstock Lode in Nevada, that a new impetus was given to immigration.

The story of the Comstock is the story of Nevada, but its effect was felt in California. In the first place, the flow of migration was reversed, many miners now re-crossing the Sierra into Nevada. But the techniques of mining differed from the placer mining of the gold rush—heavy machinery as well as a knowledge of mining and engineering was necessary. These needs led to the formation of large companies which found their financial backing in San Francisco and helped establish San Francisco as the financial center from which the mines were managed.

The mines stimulated the development of better transportation and communication. Paddlewheel steamers operated up the river between San Francisco and Sacramento and Stockton. Mule and pack trains carried freight not only within the state but also to neighboring territories, and after 1849 stage lines operated within the state. There was a need, however, for faster communication with the east, especially since California had become a state in 1850; but because negotiations for transcontinental stage routes and lines became involved in politics, their establishment was delayed. The first such stage route, established in 1857, ran from San Antonio to San Diego, "from nowhere to nowhere" in the opinion of Northern Californians.[12] In 1858 the Butterfield Overland Mail started, but it was unpopular with Northern Californians from the beginning because it came by the long southern route of the Gila Trail from Memphis (the postmaster-general at the time being from Tennessee). In 1861 the effects of the Civil War began to be felt, and the southern route was given up in favor of a central one from St. Louis by way of Salt Lake to California. Eight years later the transcontinental railroad was completed with the

[10] Caughey, p. 246.

[11] Rolle, p. 225.

[12] Rolle, p. 358.

driving of the golden spike at Promontory, Utah, at the meeting of the Central Pacific and Union Pacific railroads. The historic isolation of California was broken.

By 1875 the Southern Pacific Railroad had extended its lines from San Francisco down the San Joaquin Valley to Los Angeles, and on to New Orleans by 1883. Several towns in the San Joaquin Valley were established as a direct result.

The Santa Fe Railroad from Kansas City to Los Angeles was completed in 1887, and a branch line from Barstow to San Francisco ended the Southern Pacific monopoly of railroads in the state.

The new transportation systems opened the way for 70,000 people a year to migrate to California—at first mostly to Northern California. But in the 1880's the pattern changed and the boom was on for Southern California. Between 1880 and 1890 the population of Los Angeles increased 500 percent; Los Angeles county increased from 33,381 to 101,454, and California as a whole increased from 860,000 to 1,213,298 during the same period.[13]

With the development of irrigation in Southern California (the reclamation of Imperial Valley in 1900 and the Owens Valley aqueduct which brought water to Los Angeles in 1904) the increase in farm population continued. The finding of oil on Signal Hill at Long Beach brought others to the state in 1921, and the migration is still going on, encouraged by the development of manufacturing and industry since World War II.

Nevada

The exploration and settlement of Nevada was even later and slower than that of California. The first European in Nevada was probably Father Francisco Garcés, who came from Sonora in 1775 with de Anza. (Father Garcés is given credit by some for originating the Old Spanish Trail.)[14] In 1825 Peter Skeen Ogden of the Hudson's Bay Company first saw the Humboldt River, and thereafter many American trappers came into the territory, among them Jedediah Smith, of whom mention has already been made.

Nevada was at that time part of the Utah Territory, and the Mormons were among the first to attempt permanent settlement in the western part. As early as 1846 a party of about 200 Mormons under the leadership of

[13] C. M. Zierer, ed., *California and the Southwest* (New York, 1956), p. 121.

[14] A. L. Scott, Chapter LII, "Lincoln County," Sam P. Davis, ed., *The History of Nevada* (Reno, 1918), p. 927.

Sam Brannan had landed in San Francisco, planning to travel east to Salt Lake to join Brigham Young's people. In the same year the Mormon Battalion, consisting of five companies, left Council Bluffs for California as part of General Kearney's Army of the West. From Santa Fe they traveled south and, being then under the leadership of Colonel Philip Cooke, pioneered the cut-off to the Gila Trail which carries Cooke's name. After great hardships they reached San Diego. Many of these men, after completing their year of enlistment, returned with their families to the area of San Bernardino, where in 1851 there were about five hundred Mormons. Colonists were sent out to Nevada in 1855-1856, and at one time the Mormon empire extended as far as San Bernardino on the southwest and Genoa, Nevada, south and west of Carson City near the present California border. In 1857 Brigham Young recalled the colonists in western Nevada and San Bernardino to help protect Salt Lake City, and thereafter only eastern Nevada remained under the influence of the Mormons.

The discovery of the Comstock Lode, which became publicly known in 1859, changed the nature of the settlement of Nevada. The Mormon settlers were essentially agriculturists, not miners, and took little interest in the development of mines in the state. The influx of miners into the state not only increased the population but changed the character of it. The newcomers were not so interested in making a permanent home as they were in "striking it rich." By 1860 the population figures showed 6,102 male white, 710 female white, and 45 colored. About one-third were foreign born, mainly English, Irish, and German, and most of the population was occupied in mining.[15]

These later Nevadans, who were not Mormons, desired to be separated from the Utah Territory, and in 1861 the Territory of Nevada was organized. Again the effect of the Civil War is seen, as the wealth of Nevada was welcomed by the federal government, and Nevada became a state in 1864.

Transportation in Nevada developed as part of the transcontinental route to California. Several short railroads were developed in the state to connect the mines to the mills, one of the most important being the Virginia and Truckee Railroad, connecting the Comstock with the Central Pacific Railroad at Reno.

Although Nevada's population grew substantially after the finding of the Comstock Lode in 1859 and the development of copper mines in White Pine County on the eastern border after 1900 (42,491 in 1870; 62,266 in

[15] H. H. Bancroft, *History of Nevada, Colorado, and Wyoming,* in *The Works,* Vol. XXV (San Francisco, 1890), p. 168, note 55.

1880 and by 1910, 81,875), it still ranks today (1960 census figures) as the forty-ninth state in population, although seventh in size.

Next to mining, cattle raising was the most important industry in the state, but, because of lack of water, farming was limited to raising food for local supply only. Much of Nevada's present-day prosperity is the result of liberal divorce and gambling laws, which have helped to make tourists its biggest business.

Table 2

Approximate Dates of Modern Settlement of Communities
Used in the Linguistic Atlas of the Pacific Coast

CALIFORNIA

Most of the following information was taken from Erwin G. Gudde's California Place Names (Berkeley, 1960). It is difficult to place the date exactly for many of the towns, but this listing at least shows an approximation and a relationship to the growth of population. For those communities that were once part of the Spanish settlements (missions, etc.) a date significant to the American period has been given. The numbers in the right-hand column are the numbers assigned to the communities for the purposes of the atlas, as shown on map 21 in chapter IV.

1770	Monterey	53
1841	San Rafael (town)	41
1847	San Francisco (name)	1
1847	Los Angeles (occupation)	2
c. 1845	Stockton	5
c. 1846	Santa Ana (modern city, 1869)	69
1847	Benicia	37
1848	Sacramento	4
c. 1848	Auburn	30
1848	Napa	32
1848	Placerville	35
1848	Sonora	44
1849	Santa Cruz (town)	47
c. 1849	Mariposa	51
c. 1849	Marysville	28
1850	San Luis Obispo (town)	62
1850	Santa Barbara (incorp.)	64

1850	Oakland	3
1850	Eureka	15
1850	Red Bluff	19
1850	Chico (modern, 1860)	22
1850	Colusa	27
1850	San Diego (new town)	10
1850	San Jose (incorp.)	7
1851	San Bernardino	9
1851	Yreka	12
1851	Santa Rosa	31
1851	Petaluma	36
1852	Jackson	39
1852	Watsonville	48
1853	Alameda	3
1853	Crescent City	11
1854	Susanville	20
1854	Quincy	23
1855	Woodland	34
1857	Anaheim	67
1857	Fort Bragg (town, 1885)	21
1859	Salinas (post office)	52
1859	Lakeport	25
1859	Point Arena	24
1859	Porterville Stage Depot (town, 1864)	58
1860	Elsinore Stage Depot (town, c. 1883)	73
c. 1860	Bishop	56
c. 1860	Kelseyville	26
c. 1860	Walnut Creek (post office)	42
1861	Markleeville	40
1863	San Mateo (Southern Pacific; land grants 1836-1846)	6
1863	Menlo Park (Southern Pacific)	6
1863-4	Truckee (Southern Pacific)	29
1866	Berkeley	3
1868	Bakersfield	60
1869	Niles	45
1869	Riverside	68
1869	Lodi (Southern Pacific)	38
1870	Dixon	33
1870	Modesto (Southern Pacific)	46
1872	Redding (south of present site c. 1861)	16

1872	Burney	17
1872	Merced (Southern Pacific)	50
1872	Tulare (Southern Pacific)	59
1872	Fresno (Southern Pacific)	8
1874	Alturas	13
1874	Santa Maria	63
1875	Pomona	66
1876	Mojave	71
1876	Indio (Southern Pacific)	76
1877	Hanford (Southern Pacific)	57
1878	Brentwood	43
1880	Selma (Southern Pacific)	55
1883	Oceanside	74
1884	Banning	70
1885	Scotia	18
1886	Barstow (Southern Pacific; known as Fishpond, a stopping place for travelers in the 1860's)	72
1887	Newman (Southern Pacific)	49
1887	Dunsmuir	14
1888	Coalinga (Southern Pacific)	54
1889	Mill Valley (sawmill in 1834)	41
1898	Hemet	75
1898	Oxnard	65
c. 1905	El Centro	78
1908	Blythe	77
1909	Taft	61

NEVADA

Information for Nevada settlement was taken from Origin of Place Names (Reno, 1941), Federal Writers' Project; from H. H. Bancroft's History of Nevada (San Francisco, 1890); and from The History of Nevada, edited by Sam P. Davis (Reno, 1913). I am indebted to June Rumery McKay, who conducted the field interviews in Alamo, for the approximate date of the founding of that town.

1850	Winnemucca (as a trading station; first called French('s) Ford)	81
1851	Carson City (as a trading station)	86
c. 1850-55	Wells	83
1855	Las Vegas (as a way station in 1852)	95
1859	Reno (a hotel on the site at this time; first called Fuller's Crossing, then Lake's Crossing or Bridge; officially established by the Central Pacific R.R. in 1868)	85
1861	Lovelock	84
1861	Yerington (first called Pizen Switch, then Greenfield, finally Yerington)	89
1862-3	Austin	88
1868-9	Elko	82
1869	Pioche	93
1881	Hawthorne	90
1885	Ely (mining district in 1868)	92
1896	Fallon	87
1900	Tonopah	91
c. 1906	Alamo	94

COMPOSITION OF THE POPULATION

California

The graphs in table 3 illustrate the growth and characteristics of the California population from 1860 to 1960.[16]

From the 1870 census it is found that the five states which contributed the greatest number of people to California were New York, Ohio, Missouri, Massachusetts, and Maine. Natives from all of these five states were found in every county of California except Mono, where there were none from Missouri. Maps indicating those counties which showed over 10 percent of the population from each of these states are included, following two maps which show the percentage (by counties) of the total population born in other parts of the United States. In these maps New York is represented in the largest number of counties and has the widest spread—from Del Norte to San Diego—with Missouri next. In eight counties (Del Norte, Trinity, Placer, Sacramento, Calaveras, Mariposa, Inyo, and

[16] R. W. Durrenberger, Patterns on the Land (Woodland Hills, California, 1965). Used by permission of the present publishers, National Press Books, Palo Alto, California.

POPULATION CHARACTERISTICS

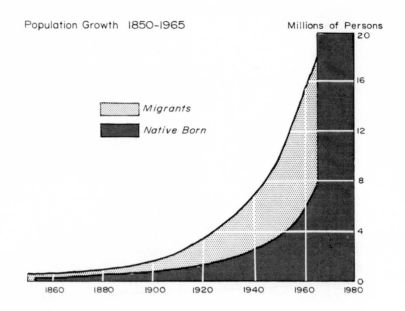

Population Growth 1850-1965

Millions of Persons

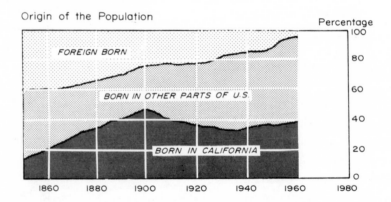

Origin of the Population

Percentage

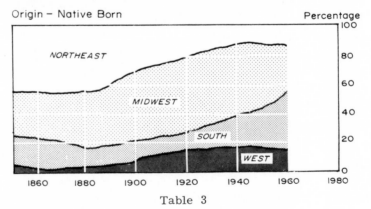

Origin – Native Born

Percentage

Table 3

San Diego) New York was the only state to contribute 10 percent or more. Likewise, in seven counties (Mendocino, Lake, Colusa, Stanislaus, Fresno, Tulare, and San Luis Obispo) Missouri was the only one of over 10 percent, although New York counted between 9.5 and 9.9 percent in Mendocino, Lassen, and Stanislaus counties. Also to be noted is the fact that San Francisco had over 10 percent from only New York and Massachusetts (maps 6, 8-12).

By 1880, Illinois and Pennsylvania were contributing greater numbers than Maine, and immigrants from Iowa and Indiana were numerous enough to be listed in the census breakdown by the counties, but no county had as much as 10 percent of its population from these two states. Illinois settlers were in much the same areas as those from Missouri, Pennsylvanians as Ohioans. Also, by 1880 New York contributed over 10 percent to San Luis Obispo, Stanislaus, and Kern counties together with Missouri, but Missouri remained the only one contributing 10 percent or more in Fresno, Tulare, and Lake counties, while joining New York in Mariposa County (maps 7, 13, 14).

To sum up, New York contributed the largest number of immigrants, widely scattered over the state. Missouri was next, with special concentration in Lake and Colusa counties in the north, and Fresno and Tulare counties in the south, and generally in the Central Valley and contiguous coastal areas, but in only Lassen and Amador counties in the Sierra region. Ohio immigrants were to be found mainly north and east of the Sacramento River, Maine south of San Francisco Bay and in parts of the Sierra, and Massachusetts in the San Francisco Bay Area. It must be emphasized, however, that these generalities relate to the 10 percent figure and that <u>every</u> county had settlers from all of these states and many others, together with many from foreign countries.

It should be noted that the following counties were formed after 1879 from already existing counties in California:

Modoc from Klamath (Klamath was divided between Modoc and Siskiyou)

Glenn from Colusa

San Benito from Monterey

Madera from Fresno

Kings from Tulare

Ventura from Santa Barbara and Los Angeles

Orange from Los Angeles

Riverside from San Bernardino and San Diego

Imperial from San Diego

Similarly, in Nevada:

Mineral from Esmeralda

Pershing from Humboldt

Eureka from Lander

Clark from Lincoln

Roop was annexed to Washoe in 1883, making one county out of two.

Map 6

Population percentage 1870

Map 7

Population percentage 1880

Map 8

Population percentage from New York 1870

Map 9

Population percentage from Missouri 1870

Map 10

Population percentage from Ohio 1870

Map 11

Population percentage from Maine 1870

Map 12

Population percentage from Massachusetts 1870

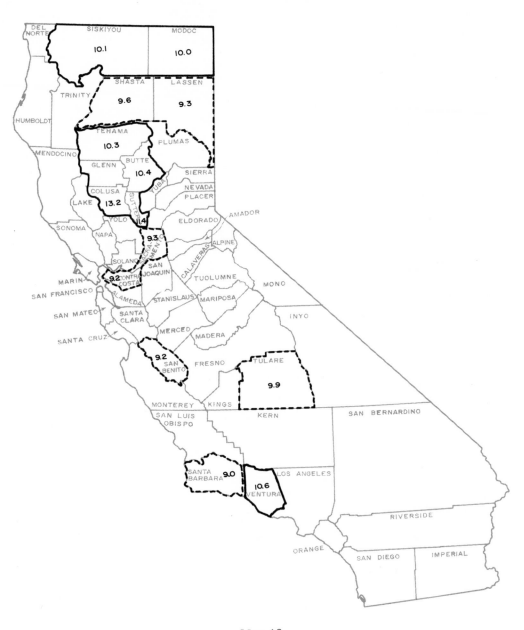

Map 13

Population percentage from Illinois 1880

Map 14

Population percentage from Pennsylvania 1880

Nevada

In Nevada in 1870, again we find New York contributed the greatest number, New Yorkers making up 10 percent or more of the population of every county in Nevada. California was next, with numbers over 10 percent found in the counties bordering on California from Inyo-Esmeralda north, and in White Pine County on the eastern border (a region with a great deal of mining activity, not only in gold and silver but, later, in copper). Ohio settlers were rather widely scattered, over 9.5 percent in all counties except Lander-Eureka and Lincoln-Clark. And in two counties, Douglas and Roop (which was annexed to Washoe in 1883), Illinois contributed over 10 percent (maps 15-19).

By 1880 New York still accounted for over 10 percent of the population of every county, and California in all but White Pine and Lincoln, where Utah now accounted for 11.3 percent in White Pine (California was 9.4 percent) and 29.2 percent in Lincoln. The only other states so represented were Ohio in Humboldt County, and Maine and Pennsylvania in Churchill County, Illinois percentages having dropped (maps 15 and 20).

Just as it was with California, it is important to remember that all of these states were represented in every county to some extent.

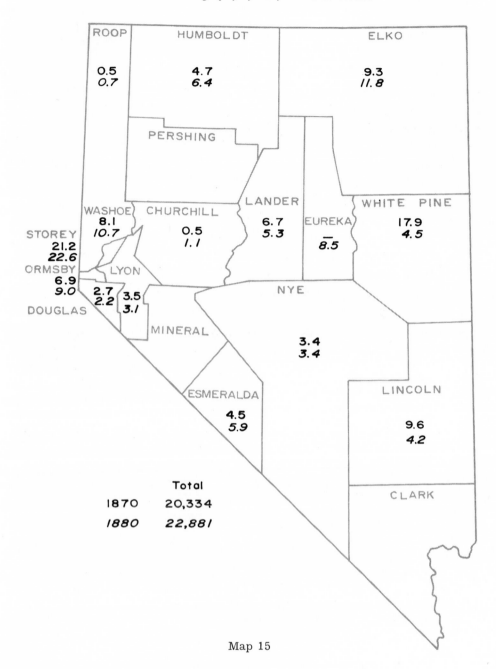

ROOP

0.5
0.7

HUMBOLDT

4.7
6.4

ELKO

9.3
11.8

PERSHING

WASHOE
8.1
10.7

CHURCHILL

0.5
1.1

LANDER

6.7
5.3

EUREKA

8.5

WHITE PINE

17.9
4.5

STOREY
21.2
22.6

ORMSBY
6.9
9.0

LYON

2.7
2.2

3.5
3.1

DOUGLAS

NYE

3.4
3.4

MINERAL

ESMERALDA

4.5
5.9

LINCOLN

9.6
4.2

CLARK

Total
1870   20,334
1880   22,881

Map 15

Population percentage 1870 and 1880

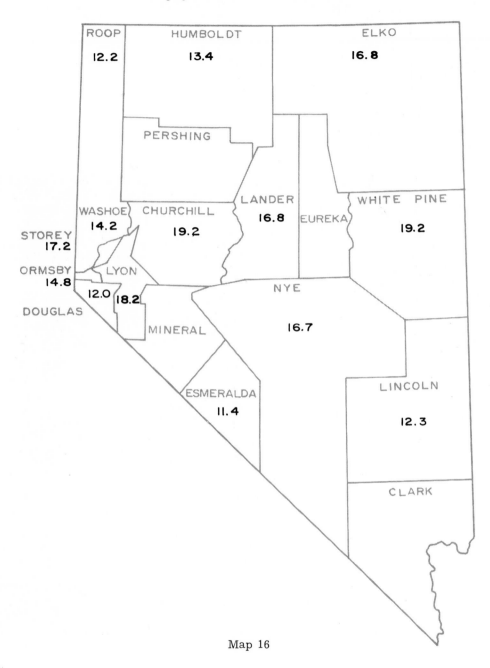

ROOP
12.2

HUMBOLDT
13.4

ELKO
16.8

PERSHING

LANDER
16.8

WHITE PINE
19.2

WASHOE
14.2

CHURCHILL
19.2

EUREKA

STOREY
17.2

ORMSBY
14.8

LYON

NYE
16.7

12.0 18.2

DOUGLAS

MINERAL

ESMERALDA
11.4

LINCOLN
12.3

CLARK

Map 16

Population percentage from New York 1870

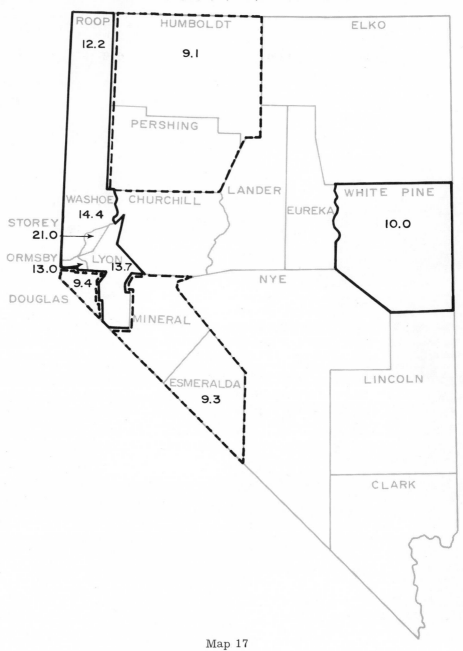

Map 17

Population percentage from California 1870

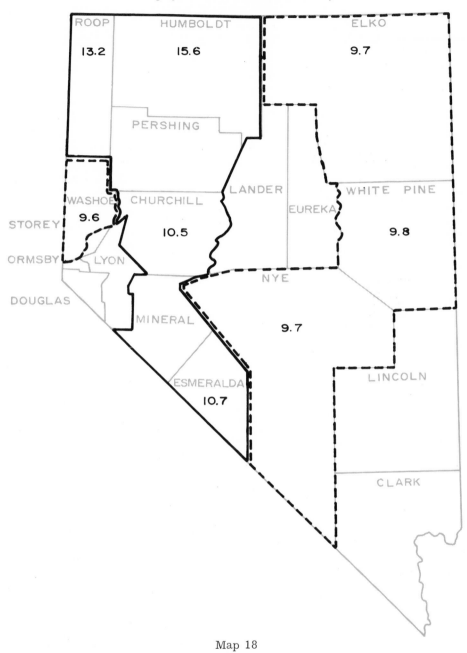

Map 18

Population percentage from Ohio 1870

Map 19

Population percentage from Illinois 1870

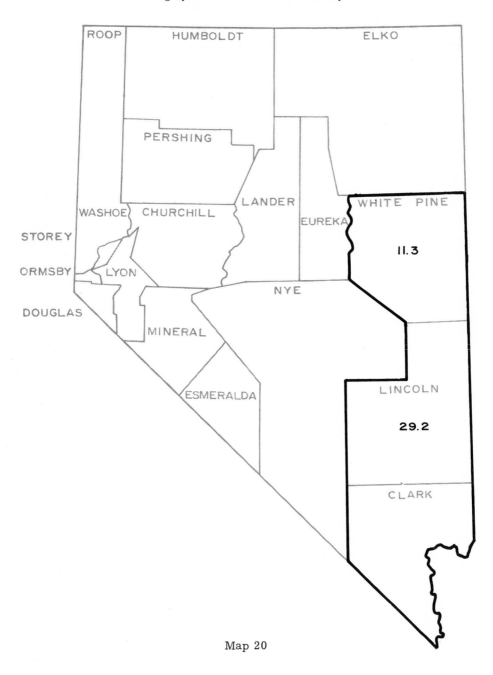

Map 20

Population percentage from Utah 1880

Chapter III

ANALYSIS OF THE CALIFORNIA-NEVADA VOCABULARY

The pattern of migration to California differed in one basic characteristic from the earlier migratory movements from the east coast westward. In the East, people from one area tended to move along the same paths and settle in generally the same areas farther west. For example, the northern Great Lakes region was settled largely by immigrants from the northern sections of the East—New England and New York state. In contrast, after the discovery of gold in California, people from all parts of the United States converged on one area, commingled and spread from there throughout the state. This first wave of migration centered in the Sacramento area and the foothills of the Sierra. San Francisco, situated as it is on the bay into which the Sacramento River empties, was the center of communication with the outside world and the center for business and finance, although Monterey had long been important in the life of California, especially as the seat of government. As the gold fever diminished, many immigrants decided to become permanent settlers and scattered throughout the state, seeking suitable sites for permanent homes. The spread, then, was away from the central area, north and south in the Central Valley, and westward to the coastal areas. In the San Joaquin Valley, this movement toward the south was a reversal of the original direction of migration with respect to the southern routes. Another reversal was seen in the movement of migrants from California to Nevada after the discovery of the Comstock Lode.

Because there was this difference in the background of settlement, together with a certain amount of grouping by state origins, as shown in chapter III, this study includes not only isoglosses of word usage that separate one area from another, but also a list of those words which came into general usage. In addition it is sometimes just as important to show where certain groups of words were not used as where they were (e.g., Patterns I-VI) in order to show the direction of spread. Therefore it is necessary to keep these different points of view in mind in order to get a sense of the spread of usage as well as to pinpoint the regionalisms and localisms, and finally to relate this region to the national picture.

From the blending of various regional speech dialects evolved a general vocabulary which can be sifted from the thousands of responses elicited for the atlas. (As an example of the variety of responses, for the one item chest of drawers twenty-one different words were elicited, only five of which occurred with enough frequency to be used in this study.) This general vocabulary includes words that occurred in at least 15 percent of the responses—a percentage which often seemed to mark the break between general distribution and regional or local distribution. Items of general usage and distribution are marked "General California-Nevada" (G. C.-N., or simply G.C. for those words that are general in California but limited in Nevada.) Those words which are labeled "Minor General Distribution" (M.G.D.) are words which have almost as wide a geographical spread but occur in lesser density or do not appear in every area. Those marked "Scattered" (S.) occur in comparatively small amounts and in widely scattered areas, with no particular pattern of distribution.

The percentages are figured on a total of 300 (the total number of informants), but the total of percentages for each item will not add up to 100 percent for several reasons: 1. Some informants gave more than one response for a single item. 2. Some informants had no response at all for some items. 3. Some answers which were suggested by the field worker or were known only by hearsay were not counted. In the case of suggested items, if the informant gave some pertinent remark which indicated that he knew the meaning and often used the word, the item was counted.

In addition to this general vocabulary, nineteen groups of words—fifteen in California and four in Nevada—occur in geographical patterns that seem to reflect several influences on word usage:

1. Spread of usage by historical migratory routes.
2. Limitation of usage to areas of earliest settlement, indicating perhaps a growing obsolescence of these items.
3. Urban-rural relationships.
4. Influence of San Francisco and Los Angeles as focal areas.

The isogloss maps and the distribution density information of the nineteen groups of words given in the tables illustrate the effects of these influences on the California-Nevada speech. Each item in the vocabulary that occurs in one of these patterns is so marked, that is, P. I, P. II, etc. (The term "pattern" has been used to cover the entire group of words because, while each word exhibits the characteristic of the isogloss boundary, there is sometimes a great difference in the extent of distribution or number of responses for some of the items within the pattern.)

Two categories are considered separately: borrowings and folk terms. Borrowings which occurred in large enough amounts are included not only in the general patterns, but also in a separate section along with other borrowings which occurred in only scattered instances. Because of the historical background of early Spanish and Mexican domination, words of Spanish origin have been treated separately from those of other sources in order that the effect of the imposition of one language on another can be evaluated.

The final section consists of folk terms which, although usually not occurring in large amounts, are of interest because of their origins, the folk myths connected with them, or their patterns of distribution.

Geographical distribution probably has less significance in analysis of grammatical forms than social factors such as the age, education, and social background of the informant—areas which are outside the scope of this study. For this reason and because of the difficulty of eliciting natural responses for items of grammar, words in this category are found only in the general vocabulary.

The complete listing of the vocabulary is given at the conclusion of the text. The items are listed in the same order as in the work sheets and the field records, with the same identifying numbers. These numbers have been used throughout the text in order to enable the reader to cross check and find not only the one item but the category to which it belongs in the general vocabulary. In addition, the context in which the item was to be used by the field workers is given to introduce each group, and a discussion of the meanings given by the informants follows. Also, the distribution pattern of each item is noted, again for purposes of cross-checking.

Table 4

Communities of the Linguistic Atlas of the Pacific Coast

Urban

The urban communities and the number of informants from each are (map 21):

1. San Francisco	25	6. Peninsula	5
2. Los Angeles	55	7. San Jose	3
3. East Bay	20	8. Fresno	3
4. Sacramento	5	9. San Bernardino	4
5. Stockton	3	10. San Diego	8

Rural

Rural areas have been divided into geographical regions on the basis of the following considerations:

1. Natural geographic boundaries (see chapter I).
2. Patterns that emerged from the study of distributions.
3. Ease of discussion.

Unless otherwise indicated, each community was represented by two informants. The geographical divisions with the communities found in each are listed below (maps 21 and 22).

North Border:

11. Crescent City
12. Yreka
13. Alturas

North Coast:

15. Eureka
18. Scotia
21. Fort Bragg
24. Point Arena

Clear Lake:

25. Lakeport
26. Kelseyville

North Bay:

31. Santa Rosa
32. Napa
36. Petaluma
41. Marin

Contra Costa:

42. Walnut Creek
43. Brentwood
45. Niles

Sacramento Valley:

14. Dunsmuir
16. Redding
17. Burney
19. Red Bluff
22. Chico
27. Colusa
28. Marysville
33. Dixon
34. Woodland
37. Benicia

Sierra:

20. Susanville
23. Quincy
29. Truckee
30. Auburn
35. Placerville
39. Jackson
40. Markleeville
44. Sonora
51. Mariposa
56. Bishop
58. Porterville

San Joaquin Valley:

38. Lodi
46. Modesto
49. Newman
50. Merced
54. Coalinga
55. Selma
57. Hanford
59. Tulare
60. Bakersfield (3)
61. Taft

Central Coast:

47. Santa Cruz
48. Watsonville
52. Salinas
53. Monterey
62. San Luis Obispo
63. Santa Maria

South Coast:

64. Santa Barbara
65. Oxnard
74. Oceanside

Pomona:

66. Pomona (3)
67. Anaheim
69. Santa Ana

Riverside:

68. Riverside (3)
70. Banning
73. Elsinore
75. Hemet

Desert: North:

71. Mojave
72. Barstow

Desert: South:

76. Indio
77. Blythe
78. El Centro

Nevada: North:

81. Winnemucca
82. Elko
83. Wells
84. Lovelock
85. Reno
86. Carson City
87. Fallon
88. Austin
89. Yerington
90. Hawthorne
91. Tonopah

Nevada: South:

92. Ely
93. Pioche
94. Alamo
95. Las Vegas

Benicia (37), Porterville (58), Oceanside (74), Banning (70), Blythe (77), Tonopah (91), and Ely (92) are borderline communities often showing characteristics of two areas.

Crescent City
Yreka
Alturas
Dunsmuir
Wells
Winnemucca
Elko
Eureka
Burney
Scotia
Redding
Susanville
Lovelock
Red Bluff
Quincy
Chico
Ft. Bragg
Reno
Fallon
Austin
Colusa
Truckee
Ely
Lakeport
Marysville
Carson City
Pt.
Arena
Kelseyville
Auburn
Yerington
Woodland
Placerville
Markleeville
Santa Rosa
Sacramento
Dixon
Hawthorne
Petaluma
Napa
Jackson
Benicia
Lodi
Marin
Brentwood
Stockton
Sonora
Tonopah
Pioche
East Bay
San Francisco
Walnut Creek
Peninsula
Niles
Modesto
Newman
Mariposa
Alamo
San Jose
Merced
Santa Cruz
Bishop
Watsonville
Salinas
Fresno
Monterey
Selma
Hanford
Las Vegas
Tulare
Coalinga
Porterville
Bakersfield
San Luis Obispo
Taft
Santa Maria
Mojave
Barstow
Santa Barbara
Oxnard
Los Angeles
San Bernardino
Pomona
Riverside
Banning
Anaheim
Hemet
Santa Ana
Elsinore
Indio
Blythe
Oceanside
El Centro
San Diego

LINGUISTIC ATLAS
of the
PACIFIC COAST COMMUNITIES

Urban
Rural

Map 21

NORTH BORDER

NORTH COAST

SACRAMENTO VALLEY

NORTH NEVADA

CLEAR LAKE

NORTH BAY

SIERRA

SOUTH NEVADA

CONTRA COSTA

SAN JOAQUIN VALLEY

CENTRAL COAST

NORTH DESERT

SOUTH COAST

POMONA

RIVERSIDE

GEOGRAPHIC AREAS
for
DISTRIBUTION STUDY

SOUTH DESERT

Map 22

For each pattern there are two items: (1) a map showing the isogloss boundaries (2) a table giving a list of the words in the group and the density of distribution by urban communities and rural geographic areas. The maps illustrate the distribution of four typical words that form the isogloss boundary, each word being represented by a symbol. The exact number of responses for each community is shown for urban areas: by the number of responses plus the symbol, and for rural areas: by one symbol for each response. In the tables the lists of words which exhibit characteristics of the isogloss also indicate other patterns in which each word may occur—the plus sign (+) for secondary isoglosses, roman numerals for patterns—and the density of distribution information shows the percentages of total possible responses given in each area for the group of words as a whole. For example, for San Francisco, on 10 items, the total possible answers would be 25 informants χ 10 items or 250 possible answers. If 50 answers were actually given, then the percentage of usage in San Francisco would be 20 percent. In a rural area of three communities with two informants in each, such as Contra Costa, the total possible answers would be 6 informants χ 10 items or 60 possible answer

Each of these sets, or in some instances, groups of related sets are preceded by a discussion of the salient characteristics of the isogloss and the factors that may have influenced usage as reflected in the isogloss.

PATTERNS I THROUGH V

Patterns I through V illustrate the spread of usage in Southern California, together with the isolation of the coastal area between Monterey and San Diego. In Pattern I occurrence in Southern California is in the Desert area only; in II the spread is in the Desert and Riverside areas; III shows the Desert, Riverside, and Pomona areas affected; IV covers the Desert and Riverside areas and Oceanside in the South Coastal area; and in V the spread is completed to all four of these, with the coastal area from San Luis Obispo to Oxnard remaining outside the boundaries of this spread, even though, otherwise, all areas of California and Nevada are covered (maps 23-27).

In all five patterns the Northern California limits are much the same, extending to Monterey on the coast and down the San Joaquin Valley inland. However, we do find a secondary isogloss, indicated by broken lines, in the valley and the central part of Nevada, in which some of the items

do not appear—an isogloss rather uncertain in boundary lines and somewhat deceiving in its appearance. From the outline, one might suppose
this to be a single area spreading across California and Nevada, but
more probably, because of the intervening Sierra Nevada and the arid
nature of the Nevada region, it is to be considered as two distinct reflec-
tions: one in California, where the lines of usage follow the San Joaquin
Valley north and south; the other in Nevada, reflecting the slowness of
spread through the sparsely settled desert areas. In addition to this
secondary isogloss, remnants of Central California exceptions (see Pattern VI) are also apparent to varying degrees north of Monterey. In the
secondary as in the primary isoglosses, the decreasing of the nonpartici-
pating areas between I and V gives us some idea of the paths of settlement (maps 28 and 29).

These patterns show the core of the vocabulary to be centered in the
area of heaviest migration from the east, that is, across northern Nevada
and the Sierra to Sacramento and the gold fields in the foothills, as well
as on down the Sacramento River to the San Francisco Bay Area. Greater
participation of the North Coast is seen in IV. Three factors which affected
the spread through the San Joaquin Valley may also be apparent: first, the
early migration via the Gila Trail and north across Tejon Pass (see map
5); second, the reversal of this direction through the valley after the building of the Southern Pacific Railroad to the south, which resulted in the
land boom of 1880 in Southern California; third, changing the flow north
again, the increasing influence of Los Angeles as a metropolitan center.
As an example of the third, thirty-five responses of the word parkway
(27.6, P. VI) were given in Los Angeles, only one in San Francisco and
three in the East Bay, with only scattered instances north of Selma (55)
in the Central Valley. The isolation of the central part of the coast from
Santa Barbara to Monterey emphasizes the popularity of the valley route.

The proportion of words from various categories, such as farm, home,
food, and topography, seems to remain fairly constant in the five patterns.
Possibly the one exception is a slightly higher proportion of farm terms
in Pattern II, with a corresponding drop in urban percentages. However,
the percentage figures in all areas show a considerable change between
the first and the fifth groups, corresponding with the wider distribution.
Equally important, the percentage of use in Los Angeles reflects the
spread of use into the Pomona area. In Patterns I, II, and IV none of the
words is found in that part, and Los Angeles has percentages of only 7
percent, 6 percent, and 7 percent respectively. In III and V, in which
Pomona shows percentages of 20 percent and 23 percent, the Los Angeles
percentages jump to 19 percent and 15 percent.

Table 5

Pattern I

7.5	suite (of rooms)	+	
8.4	storage room	+	
8.5	tidies (up)	VI	
9.5	canopy	+	
9.6	shiplap	+	
11.8	garden	+	(only one response in Nevada)
12.6	(hay) stack	+	XVIII
12.8	hog pen	+	XVIIa
16.7	burlap bag	+	XVIIa
17.7	(two) singletrees	+	(no responses in Nevada)
18.1	half (a) load	+	
22.5	breeches	+	XVIIa
24.7	bog (and compds.)	+	XVIIa
34.6	off horse	+	
37.5	bread	+	
60.8	became sick	+	(only one response in Nevada)
62.1	died from		
71.6	taws	+	

Distribution density: Percentage of total possible answers on 18 items:

Urban:			Rural:	
1.	San Francisco	17%	North Border	3%
2.	Los Angeles	7	North Coast	13
3.	East Bay	20	Clear Lake	29
4.	Sacramento	26	North Bay	15
5.	Stockton	22	Contra Costa	20
6.	Peninsula	16	Sacramento Valley	23
7.	San Jose	16	Sierra	23
8.	Fresno	11	San Joaquin Valley	14
9.	San Bernardino	5	Central Coast	12
10.	San Diego	12	(to Monterey only)	
			South Coast	--
			Pomona	--
			Riverside	--
			North Desert	30
			South Desert	21
			North Nevada	21
			South Nevada	11

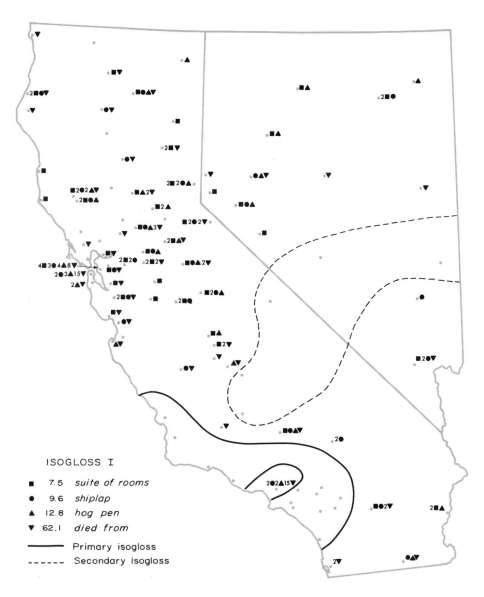

ISOGLOSS I

■   7.5   *suite of rooms*
●   9.6   *shiplap*
▲ 12.8 *hog pen*
▼ 62.1 *died from*

———— Primary isogloss
- - - - - Secondary isogloss

Map 23

Table 6

Pattern II

3.6	came/come up	+		
7.5	furniture	+		
7.7	looking glass	+	VI	
10.6	woodshed			
12.7	barn			
14.1	wooden bucket			
14.4	slop bucket	+	VI, XI	
16.7	burlap sack	VI		
	barley sack	+	VI, XVIIa	
19.7	emery wheel	+	VI	
25.2	plain(s)	+	XVIIa	
29.8	mustang			
33.3	here boss (ie)	+	XVIII	
33.5	call by name			
38.8	sourdough	+	VI	
39.7	dried beef	VI		
55.6	school boy/girl/kid/child			
56.2	cowhand	VI		
	cowpuncher			
56.8	migrant(s) (worker)	+		
57.5	look at this/that	+	VI	
60.2	set (in his ways)	+		
60.8	became ill	+	VI	XVIII
62.8	heave			
65.3	opera house	+	VI	XVIIa
67.7	S.F.	+	VI	XVIIa
69.2	pretty	+	XVIIa	
69.5	[jael]	+	XVIIa	
69.7	[hm?m/?m?m]	+		
73.1	give you a lift	+	XVIIa	
	help you (home)	+	VI	
74.4	gather	+	XVIIa	

Distribution density: Percentage of total possible answers on 32 items:

Urban:			Rural:	
1.	San Francisco	9%	North Border	10%
2.	Los Angeles	6	North Coast	28
3.	East Bay	22	Clear Lake	46
4.	Sacramento	30	North Bay	11
5.	Stockton	13	Contra Costa	24
6.	Peninsula	10	Sacramento Valley	31
7.	San Jose	4	Sierra	24
8.	Fresno	21	San Joaquin Valley	17
9.	San Bernardino	7	Central Coast	7
10.	San Diego	11	(to Monterey)	
			South Coast	1
			Pomona	--
			Riverside	20
			North Desert	28
			South Desert	28
			North Nevada	36
			South Nevada	21

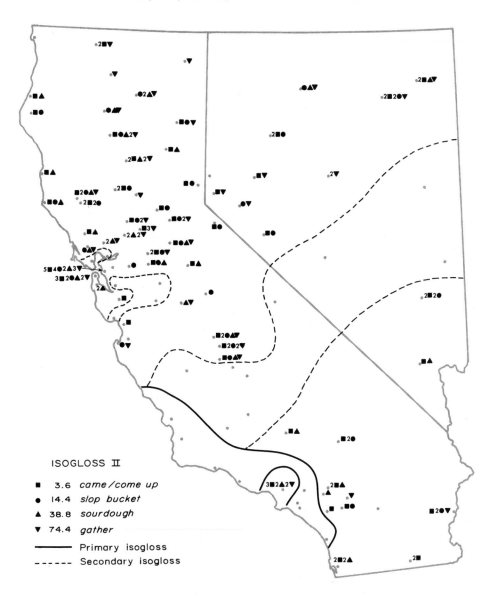

ISOGLOSS II

■	3.6	*came/come up*
●	14.4	*slop bucket*
▲	38.8	*sourdough*
▼	74.4	*gather*

——— Primary isogloss

- - - - - Secondary isogloss

Map 24

Table 7

Pattern III

2.6	at once	+	
3.5	dawn		
4.8	heavy rain		
5.8	black frost	VI	
	white frost	VI	
6.3	sitting room	+	
7.6	curtains	+	XVIIa
13.7	rock wall	+	
15.1	rinch/rench	+	VI
18.4	horse	+	XVIII
27.6	parkway		
30.7	shoes	+	XVIIb
33.2	chores (and phrases)		
44.6	seed		
46.7	green beans	+	
48.7	ground squirrel	+	
57.2	nearly fell down		
60.8	took ill/sick		

Distribution: Percentage of total possible answers on 18 items:

Urban:

1.	San Francisco	13%
2.	Los Angeles	14
3.	East Bay	18
4.	Sacramento	21
5.	Stockton	12
6.	Peninsula	10
7.	San Jose	18
8.	Fresno	12
9.	San Bernardino	9
10.	San Diego	16

Rural:

North Border	13%
North Coast	20
Clear Lake	22
North Bay	11
Contra Costa	16
Sacramento Valley	21
Sierra	20
San Joaquin Valley	14
Central Coast (to Monterey)	14
South Coast	--
Pomona	20
Riverside	20
North Desert	30
South Desert	20
North Nevada	20
South Nevada	10

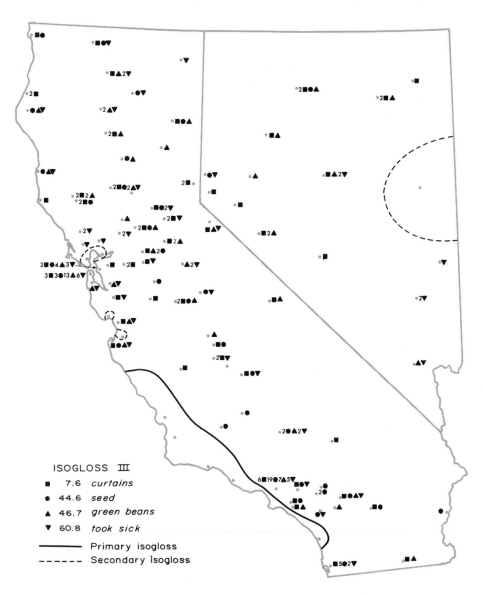

ISOGLOSS III

■ 7.6 *curtains*
● 44.6 *seed*
▲ 46.7 *green beans*
▼ 60.8 *took sick*
────── Primary isogloss
─ ─ ─ ─ Secondary isogloss

Map 25

Table 8

Pattern IV

5.8	heavy frost	+	VI, XVIII
	light frost	+	VI
23.5	coin purse	+	VI, XVIIb
25.4	plain(s)		
27.2	oil(ed) road		
31.1	donkey	+	
32.8	coop	+	
38.4	flapjacks	+	
38.5	receipt	+	XVIIa
39.7	chip beef	+	
43.1	leftover(s)/(food)	+	
43.7	jam	+	VI
	preserves	+	VI
51.7	(maple) orchard	+	VI
73.1	give you a ride	+	VI
73.4	packed	+	

Distribution density—percentage of total possible answers on 16 items:

Urban:			Rural:	
1.	San Francisco	16%	North Border	9%
2.	Los Angeles	7	North Coast	42
3.	East Bay	32	Clear Lake	45
4.	Sacramento	35	North Bay	12
5.	Stockton	18	Contra Costa	28
6.	Peninsula	18	Sacramento Valley	41
7.	San Jose	16	Sierra	33
8.	Fresno	18	San Joaquin Valley	20
9.	San Bernardino	18	Central Coast	10
10.	San Diego	7	(to Monterey)	
			South Coast	18*
			Pomona	--
			Riverside	23
			North Desert	34
			South Desert	33
			North Nevada	35
			South Nevada	21

*All responses from 74, Oceanside.

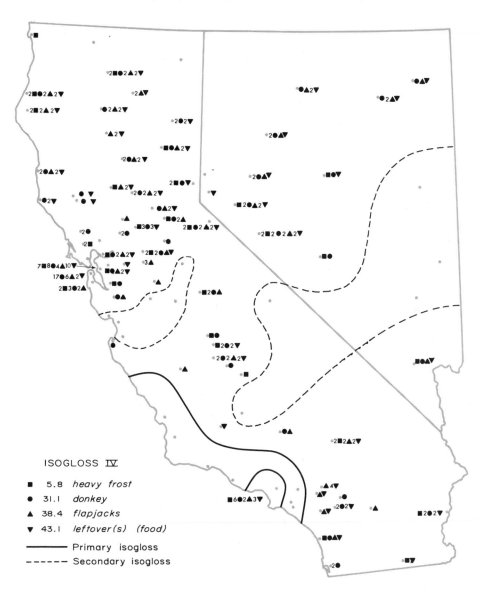

ISOGLOSS Ⅳ

- ■ 5.8 *heavy frost*
- ● 31.1 *donkey*
- ▲ 38.4 *flapjacks*
- ▼ 43.1 *leftover(s) (food)*
- ——— Primary isogloss
- - - - - Secondary isogloss

Map 26

Table 9

Pattern V

19.3	juice harp
19.4	coal scuttle/shuttle/hod
28.3	towards
31.5	sow(s) + VI
32.6	whinny
	neigh
34.8	lariat
35.2	a short way(s)
35.8	second crop
36.1	a bundle
36.2	bushel (plural)
43.3	garden
74.6	commenced

Distribution density—percentage of total possible answers on 15 items:

Urban:			Rural:	
1.	San Francisco	29%	North Border	14%
2.	Los Angeles	15	North Coast	39
3.	East Bay	42	Clear Lake	48
4.	Sacramento	45	North Bay	32
5.	Stockton	31	Contra Costa	34
6.	Peninsula	25	Sacramento Valley	39
7.	San Jose	33	Sierra	30
8.	Fresno	40	San Joaquin Valley	29
9.	San Bernardino	36	Central Coast	20
10.	San Diego	34	(to Monterey)	
			South Coast	20*
			Pomona	23
			Riverside	40
			North Desert	30
			South Desert	33
			North Nevada	40
			South Nevada	28

*All responses from 74, Oceanside.

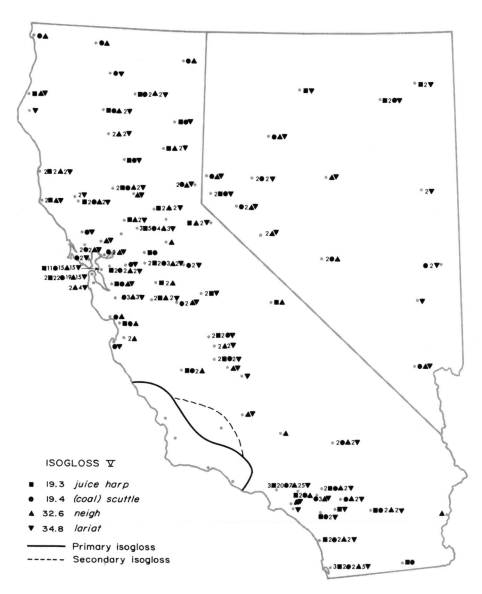

ISOGLOSS Ⅴ

■ 19.3 *juice harp*
● 19.4 *(coal) scuttle*
▲ 32.6 *neigh*
▼ 34.8 *lariat*

———— Primary isogloss
------- Secondary isogloss

Map 27

PATTERN VI

CENTRAL CALIFORNIA EXCEPTIONS

For the sake of clarity, Pattern VI is shown separately, although it is obvious that there is a close relationship in the distribution shown on maps 23 to 29 (cf. the secondary isogloss). Pattern VI shows an area in Central California east and south of San Francisco Bay in which thirty-six items did not appear. Of these thirty-six items, all but eight appear in the first five patterns. The outer limits of this area vary as shown by the shaded areas (map 29). Monterey, the early capital, shows a higher percentage of usage than other surrounding communities. Responses from the urban communities in this area (1, 3, 4, 5, 6, 7, 8) were not included in the computations.

The first six patterns, in which the central and southern coast from Monterey to San Diego are isolated from the rest of the state, are particularly interesting in view of the fact that this coastal area was the part that was settled first by the Spanish with the establishment of the missions, pueblos, and presidios. In table 27, which shows the use of Spanish borrowings, the percentage of borrowings found in Contra Costa, the Central Coast, and the South Coast areas is slightly higher than in the surrounding areas, and conversely, in the chart of Americanizations, the percentage is lower. This is the only real evidence we have of the competition between the two languages, which was obviously stronger in these areas than elsewhere.

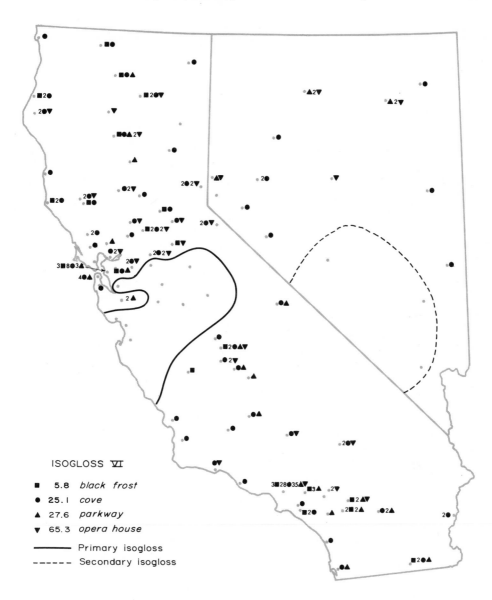

ISOGLOSS Ⅵ

■ 5.8 *black frost*
● 25.1 *cove*
▲ 27.6 *parkway*
▼ 65.3 *opera house*

⎯⎯⎯⎯⎯ Primary isogloss
------- Secondary isogloss

Map 28

Table 10

Pattern VI

3.5	sun-up	
5.8	black frost	III
	white frost	III
	heavy frost	IV
	light frost	IV
6.3	front room	
7.7	looking glass	II
8.5	tidies up	I
9.5	canopy	I
14.4	slop bucket	II
15.1	rinch/rench	III
16.7	burlap sack	II
	barley bag/sack	II
19.7	emery wheel	II
23.5	coin purse	IV
25.1	inlet	
	cove	
27.6	parkway	III
31.5	sow	V
38.8	sourdough	II
39.7	dried beef	II
43.1	leftover(s) (food)	IV
43.7	jam	IV
	preserves	IV
44.5	seed	
44.6	seed	III
49.6	horned toad	
51.7	(maple) orchard	IV
56.2	cow hand	II
57.5	look at this	II
60.8	became ill	II
65.3	opera house	II
67.7	S.F.	II
71.6	agates	
	glassies	
73.1	give you a lift	II
	give you a ride	IV
	help you home	II

Percentage of participation by communities. Except as otherwise indicated, this group of words is in general use in other areas.

Other	North Bay:	13%	50.	Merced	5%
41.	Marin	6	51.	Mariposa	7
42.	Walnut Creek	34	52.	Salinas	7
43.	Brentwood	36	53.	Monterey	19
44.	Sonora	1	54.	Coalinga	3
45.	Niles	6	55.	Selma	44
46.	Modesto	1	56.	Bishop	11
47.	Santa Cruz	1	Other	San Joaquin Valley (57-61)	18
48.	Watsonville	--			
49.	Newman	1	Other	Central Coast (62, 63)	7

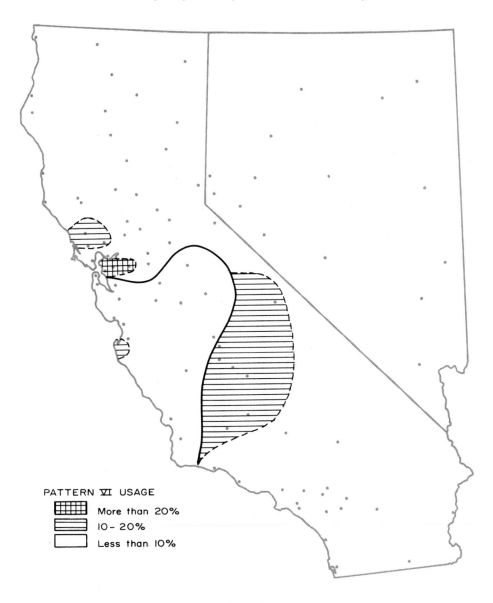

PATTERN VI USAGE

More than 20%

10 - 20%

Less than 10%

Map 29

PATTERN VII. CENTRAL CALIFORNIA AND SOUTH

Pattern VII consists of thirty items which occur in limited numbers south of a line running east and west between Truckee, Kelseyville, and the southern end of the North Coast (map 30).

The influence of Southern California in this pattern is substantiated by four facts: first, the large percentage of usage in Los Angeles and San Diego; second, the presence of two Spanish terms, adobe (and its variations) and cholo; third, several items such as dry year, desert, horny toad, which are more closely related to the climate and topography of Southern California; and finally, the presence of such innovations as wardrobe (7.8) used to mean a built-in closet, and (clothes) hamper (17.1) for laundry basket, both of which are found in Los Angeles and San Diego but not San Francisco.

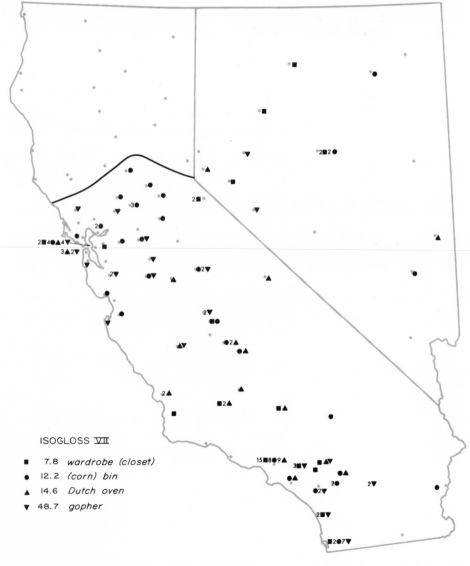

ISOGLOSS VII

■   7.8 *wardrobe (closet)*
●   12.2 *(corn) bin*
▲   14.6 *Dutch oven*
▼   48.7 *gopher*

Map 30

Table 11

Pattern VII

3.4	evening
5.4	dry year
7.7	dressing table
7.8	wardrobe (closet)
8.2	rubbish
9.3	(back) steps
9.8	(a)dobe blocks
10.7	(a)dobe bricks
	dobe
	adobe(s)
10.6	shed
12.2	(corn) bin
14.6	Dutch oven
16.4	blacksnake
17.1	(clothes) hamper
25.3	desert
29.5	leppy
35.4	the farthest
48.7	gopher
49.6	horny toad
51.3	web
51.4	web
52.8	pa
53.1	ma
54.4	illegitimate
57.1	cholo
61.7	perspired
64.2	ditched
73.1	see you (home)
	drive you (home)

Distribution density—percentage of total possible answers on 30 items:

1.	San Francisco	16%	North Border	8 %
2.	Los Angeles	20	North Coast	0.8
3.	East Bay	13	Clear Lake	1
4.	Sacramento	4	North Bay	12
5.	Stockton	21	Contra Costa	10
6.	Peninsula	12	Sacramento Valley	3
7.	San Jose	16	Sierra	12
8.	Fresno	18	San Joaquin Valley	17
9.	San Bernardino	18	Central Coast	20
10.	San Diego	24	South Coast	22
			Pomona	18
			Riverside	15
			North Desert	10
			South Desert	11
			North Nevada	13
			South Nevada	16

PATTERN VIII. NORTHERN CALIFORNIA RURAL
PATTERN IX. CENTRAL VALLEY, SIERRA AND NEVADA

Patterns VIII and IX are the most limited geographically of the predominantly rural patterns. Indications of relic areas can be seen in the use of words like burial grounds (62.2), playhouse and showhouse (both 65.3). The one informant in the North Desert who gave playhouse used it specifically to refer to the Pasadena Playhouse, in contrast to the general meaning of Northern California usage. These two patterns also show the close relation between the northern areas of Nevada and California (maps 31 and 32).

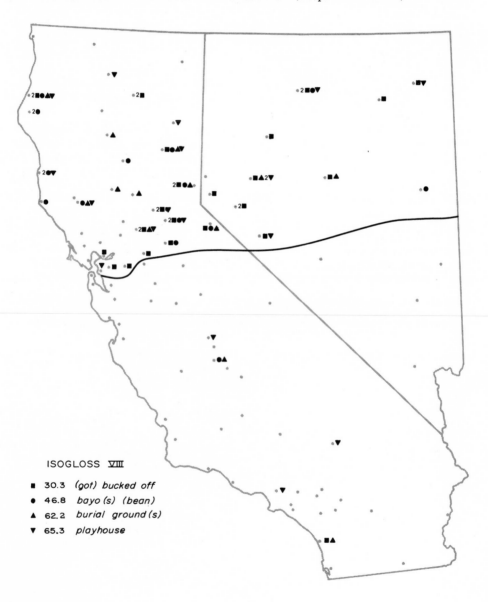

ISOGLOSS VIII

■ 30.3 *(got) bucked off*
● 46.8 *bayo (s) (bean)*
▲ 62.2 *burial ground (s)*
▼ 65.3 *playhouse*

Map 31

Table 12

Pattern VIII

2.6	(all) at one time
4.4	fifteen (minutes) to eleven
19.6	scythe stone
22.8	handkerchief
30.3	(got) bucked off
31.5	gilt(s)
34.6	nigh horse
46.8	bayo(s)
	brown beans
48.5	sapsucker
50.6	snake doctor
59.2	muscular
	powerful
60.3	peeved
	excited
62.2	burial grounds
65.3	playhouse
	showhouse
70.8	fifteen-cent store

Distribution density—percentage of total possible answers on 19 items.

1.	San Francisco	1%	North Border	2%
2.	Los Angeles	0.9	North Coast	17
3.	East Bay	0.7	Clear Lake	21
4.	Sacramento	8	North Bay	--
5.	Stockton	5	Contra Costa	26
6.	Peninsula	1	Sacramento Valley	11
7.	San Jose	3	Sierra	11
8.	Fresno	7	San Joaquin Valley	8
9.	San Bernardino	3	Central Coast	7
10.	San Diego	--	South Coast	1*
			Pomona	--
			Riverside	--
			North Desert	1+
			South Desert	--
			North Nevada	11
			South Nevada	1

*From Oceanside only.

+Response of playhouse, qualified by "in Pasadena."

Table 13

Pattern IX

18.1   small load
60.6   indolent
63.7   wed(ded)
64.4   public school
71.1   belly buster*

Distribution density—percentage of total possible answers on 5 items:

1.	San Francisco	--%	North Border	--%
2.	Los Angeles	1	North Coast	--
3.	East Bay	9	Clear Lake	--
4.	Sacramento	4	North Bay	--
5.	Stockton	--	Contra Costa	--
6.	Peninsula	--	Sacramento Valley	14
7.	San Jose	--	Sierra	16
8.	Fresno	6	San Joaquin	5
9.	San Bernardino	--	Central Coast	--
10.	San Diego	5	South Coast	3
			Pomona	--
			Riverside	--
			North Desert	--
			South Desert	--
			North Nevada	14
			South Nevada	2

*In Southern California generally used as a term in diving rather than in sledding.

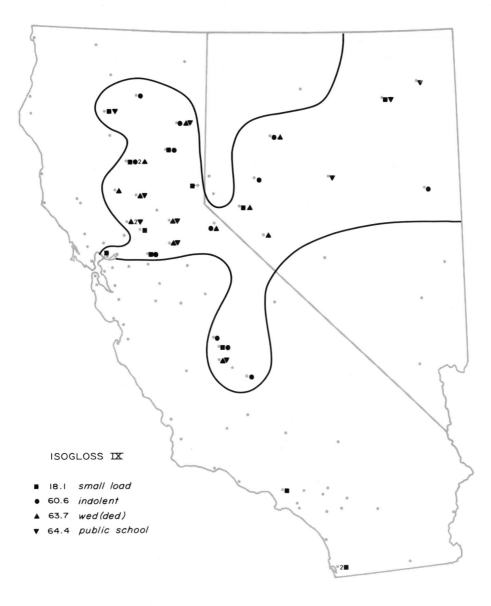

ISOGLOSS IX

- ■ 18.1 *small load*
- ● 60.6 *indolent*
- ▲ 63.7 *wed (ded)*
- ▼ 64.4 *public school*

Map 32

PATTERN X. URBAN AND NORTHERN CALIFORNIA RURAL

At first glance Pattern X, consisting of thirty-nine items, would seem to belong to one of the first five patterns. However, these items are found on the central and south coasts, and occurrences inland in Southern California are very scattered. As would be expected because of the high percentage of urban occurrence, the number of farm terms has fallen off in this pattern, but a number of words that were considered old-fashioned or obsolescent appear, e.g., <u>parlor</u> (6.3), <u>water closet</u> (11.2), and <u>face rag</u> (15.4) (map 33).

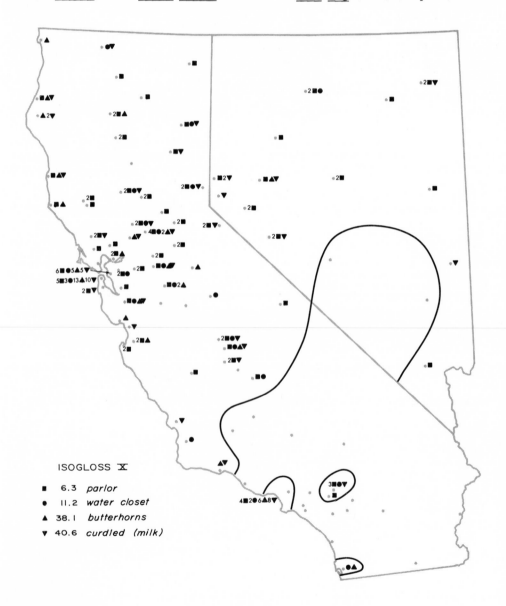

ISOGLOSS X

■	6.3	*parlor*
●	11.2	*water closet*
▲	38.1	*butterhorns*
▼	40.6	*curdled (milk)*

Map 33

Table 14

Pattern X

4.8	storm
5.1	thunder and lightning
5.6	calm down
6.2	thin coating of ice
6.3	parlor
7.4	daybed
	loveseat
8.4	junkroom
11.1	tint (total response)/(as water base paint)
11.2	water closet
11.8	lot
15.4	face cloth
	face rag
20.1	auto
	machine
26.5	gap
26.8	seawall
38.1	butterhorns
40.6	curdled (milk)
41.6	bite (to eat)
41.7	start
42.7	soda
47.3	(corn) silk
49.1	prongs
50.4	millers
50.5	glowworm
51.2	tick
53.2	family
53.3	family
56.5	coon
61.1	took cold
64.2	cut class/school
68.7	bugaboo
69.7	nope
71.6	puries
72.7	awoke
74.3	expect

Distribution density—percentage of total possible answers on 39 items:

1.	San Francisco	29%	North Border	11%
2.	Los Angeles	10	North Coast	17
3.	East Bay	16	Clear Lake	14
4.	Sacramento	18	North Bay	15
5.	Stockton	16	Contra Costa	14
6.	Peninsula	14	Sacramento Valley	15
7.	San Jose	14	Sierra	14
8.	Fresno	13	San Joaquin Valley	12
9.	San Bernardino	8	Central Coast	11
10.	San Diego	8	South Coast	5
			Pomona	--
			Riverside	1
			North Desert	1
			South Desert	0.8
			North Nevada	11
			South Nevada	8

PATTERN XI. RURAL

The largest group of words—fifty-one items—occurs in Pattern XI and is predominantly agricultural in character. The percentages of urban usage indicate that Sacramento, Fresno, and San Bernardino retain the closest relation to the rural areas, with East Bay, Stockton, San Jose, and San Diego next. San Francisco, Los Angeles, the Peninsula, and the North Bay areas maintain a more urban character (see also Patterns VII and XII) (map 34).

Also to be noted in this pattern is the reappearance of the secondary isoglosses in central California and Nevada that were found in Patterns I-VI.

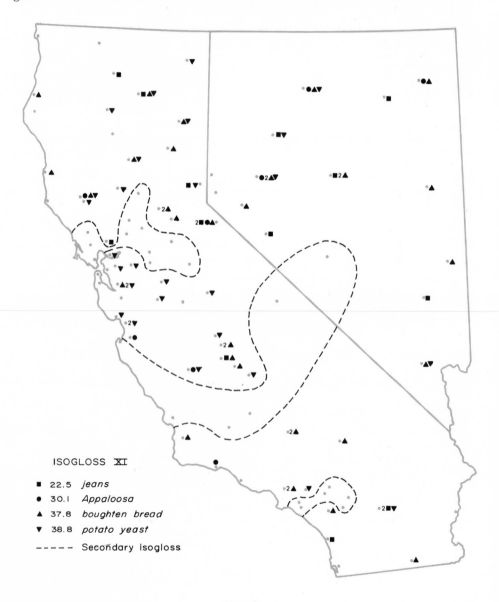

ISOGLOSS XI

■   22.5   *jeans*
●   30.1   *Appaloosa*
▲   37.8   *boughten bread*
▼   38.8   *potato yeast*

- - - - -   Secondary Isogloss

Map 34

Table 15

Pattern XI

4.7	breaking	47.2	ears of corn
6.4	chim(b)ley +		fresh corn
14.4	slop bucket/pail/can +		green corn +
	swill barrel/bucket/pail +		roasting ears
16.4	blacksnake	48.5	flicker
22.5	jeans +		yellow hammer
	overalls/___halls +	48.6	civet/civik/civvy cat
23.8	parasol +	49.7	fish(ing) worm +
24.5	pallet	50.6	mosquito hawk
29.2	sire		snake feeder
29.5	leppy	50.7 and 51.1 mud dauber +
30.1	Appaloosa	53.3	folks +
30.4	sunfishing +	56.2	buckaroo
31.5	shoat +		herdsman
32.3	bellows/bellers	56.6	rancher
	blat	56.8	fruit tramp
34.6	wheeler	57.1	nationals
	wheel horse	58.3	whiskers
36.1	shock +	60.2	ornery/onery
37.5	light bread +	63.5	sparking
37.8	boughten bread	64.1	shindig +
38.4	griddle cakes	71.6	dobabes/dobabies
38.8	start/starter of yeast		shooters
	potato yeast +		steelies
39.5	skin	74.3	figure on +
43.3	home garden		hope to +

Distribution density—percentage of total possible answers on 52 items:

1.	San Francisco	1%	North Border	6%
2.	Los Angeles	2	North Coast	16
3.	East Bay	5	Clear Lake	23
4.	Sacramento	8	North Bay	3
5.	Stockton	5	Contra Costa	19
6.	Peninsula	1	Sacramento Valley	18
7.	San Jose	5	Sierra	15
8.	Fresno	9	San Joaquin Valley	12
9.	San Bernardino	6	Central Coast	6
10.	San Diego	5	South Coast	9
			Pomona	8
			Riverside	9
			North Desert	14
			South Desert	21
			North Nevada	16
			South Nevada	9

PATTERN XII. URBAN

Only seven items were found to be predominantly urban in distribution, some rather surprisingly so, as Okies and Arkies (56.6). They also range from old-fashioned—potters' field (62.2)—to innovation—jalopy (20.1). This group is probably too small and varied to allow for any general conclusions (map 35).

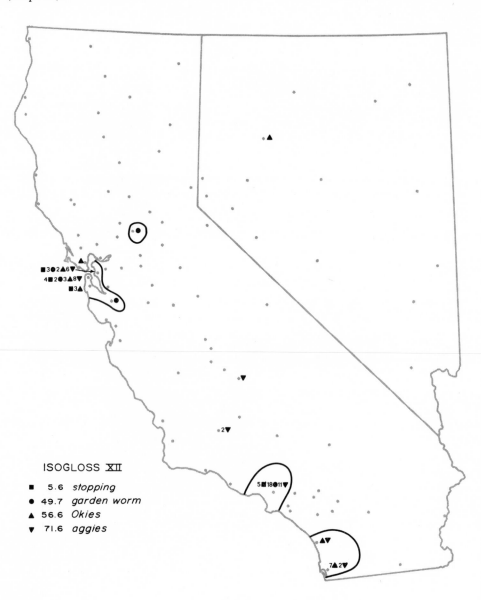

ISOGLOSS XII

■   5.6   *stopping*
● 49.7 *garden worm*
▲ 56.6 *Okies*
▼ 71.6 *aggies*

Map 35

Table 16

Pattern XII

5.6	stopping
20.1	jalopy
49.7	garden worm
56.6	Arkies
	Okies
62.2	potters' field
71.6	aggies

Distribution density—percentage of total possible answers on 7 items:

1.	San Francisco	11%	North Border	--%
2.	Los Angeles	12	North Coast	--
3.	East Bay	9	Clear Lake	--
4.	Sacramento	2	North Bay	1
5.	Stockton	--	Contra Costa	--
6.	Peninsula	11	Sacramento Valley	--
7.	San Jose	4	Sierra	0.6
8.	Fresno	--	San Joaquin Valley	1
9.	San Bernardino	--	Central Coast	1
10.	San Diego	30	South Coast	7*
			Pomona	--
			Riverside	--
			North Desert	--
			South Desert	--
			North Nevada	1
			South Nevada	--

*All from Oceanside.

PATTERN XIIIA, SAN FRANCISCO; PATTERN XIIIB,
CHESTERFIELD; PATTERN XIIIC, SAN FRANCISCO
INFLUENCE; AND PATTERN XIV, THE CITY

The items of Pattern XIIIa are limited almost entirely to San Francisco. The use of a thunder and lightning as a singular count noun was
definitely noted by the field worker (map 36).

The chesterfield isogloss, Pattern XIIIb, was first described by
Professor David W. Reed (1954): "The word chesterfield, meaning
'davenport, couch, or sofa,' and found elsewhere on this continent prin-
cipally in Canadian English, occurs in three-quarters of the question-
naires filled out in the area north of the ten southernmost counties of
California and west of the Sierra Nevada. East of the Sierra in Northern
California it appears in only one-quarter of the individual responses,
and in Southern California it is known to only one person in twenty.
I suspect that it will be found west of the mountains in Washington and
Oregon, but as yet have no proof of this"[1] (map 37).

Pattern XIIIc is made up of words that are within the chesterfield
isogloss and is therefore probably to be regarded as defining the range
of San Francisco influence. Pattern XIV is something of a reversal of
Patterns XIIIb and c, showing words that follow the pattern of the city
(67.7), a term used to refer to San Francisco (maps 38 and 39).

The range of the city pattern is almost identical with that of Pattern
XIIIc, and the percentages of usage are much the same except that those
for the Peninsula and North Bay fall considerably and there are no San
Francisco responses.

These two patterns, XIII and XIV, seemingly hold much of the history
of Northern California—the importance of the early days of the Gold
Rush and the subsequent development of San Francisco as a cosmo-
politan center exerting its influence on the surrounding areas. The
Peninsula and North Bay, developing later as settled areas, show their
affinity to the city and its influence.

[1]David W. Reed, "Eastern Dialect Words in California," Publication of the
American Dialect Society, No. 21, April, 1954, p. 5.

Table 17

Pattern XIII. San Francisco and the chesterfield Pattern XIIIa

5.1	a thunder and lightning/a lightning and thunder
25.1	creek (salt)
27.2	tar/tarred road
71.2	tumblesault

Distribution density—percentage of total possible answers on 4 items:

1.	San Francisco	35%	Clear Lake	6%
3.	East Bay	2	North Bay	6
6.	Peninsula	10	Pomona	3

No responses from other communities.

XIIIb and XIIIc—chesterfield:

7.4	chesterfield
4.4	fifteen to eleven
4.8	pourdown (noun)
5.2	tule fog
5.7	chinook (Also XVI. See vocabulary discussion.)
7.5	chesterfield set
8.3	garret
8.5	does the housework
26.5	cut
26.6	coast
27.2	tarred road
38.1	buns
	Danish pastry
46.8	cranberry beans
49.4	lobster
50.1	shiners
50.6	ear sewer
51.2	wood tick
51.8	plane tree
	Oriental plane
56.1	letter carrier
60.5	corked
62.7	yellow jaunders
63.1	vomit
64.5	primary
68.6	good God!
69.2	fairly
71.6	chinas

Distribution density for chesterfield pattern—percentage of total possible answers on 28 items:

1.	San Francisco	17%	North Border	4%
2.	Los Angeles	0.2	North Coast	5
3.	East Bay	11	Clear Lake	11
4.	Sacramento	18	North Bay	11
5.	Stockton	9	Contra Costa	12
6.	Peninsula	14	Sacramento Valley	13
7.	San Jose	8	Sierra	7
8.	Fresno	5	San Joaquin Valley	6
9.	San Bernardino	3	Central Coast	5
10.	San Diego	4	South Coast	1
			Pomona	--
			Riverside	0.3
			North Desert	2
			South Desert	0.5
			North Nevada	10
			South Nevada	5

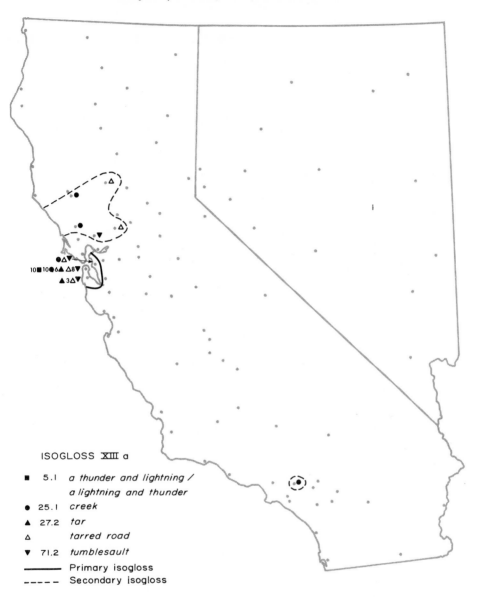

ISOGLOSS XIII a

■ 5.1   *a thunder and lightning /*
          a lightning and thunder
● 25.1 *creek*
▲ 27.2 *tar*
△   *tarred road*
▼ 71.2 *tumblesault*
———— Primary isogloss
----- Secondary isogloss

Map 36

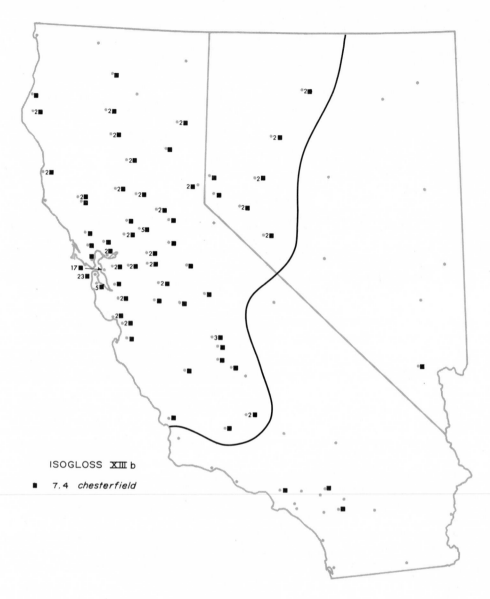

ISOGLOSS XIII b

■   7.4 *chesterfield*

Map 37

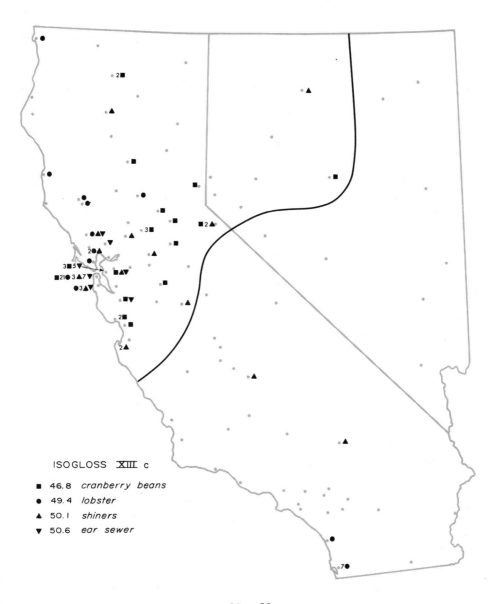

ISOGLOSS XIII c

■ 46.8 *cranberry beans*
● 49.4 *lobster*
▲ 50.1 *shiners*
▼ 50.6 *ear sewer*

Map 38

Table 18

Pattern XIV. the city

67.7	the city
6.2	coat(ing) (of ice)
9.6	rustic (siding)
11.8	lawn
19.5	wheel barrel
24.8	slough
	tulies and compounds
25.2	desert
45.8	pine nuts
50.3	timber rattler
54.4	catch colt
56.3	roustabout
	chore man
60.3	hot (around/under the collar)
63.5	calling on
63.7	tied (the knot) (up)
63.8	reception
64.1	hoedown
67.7	San Fran
70.8	notion store
	novelty store
71.6	crystal
74.1	frame of mind

Distribution density—percentage of total possible answers on 23 items:

1.	San Francisco	--%	North Border	4%
2.	Los Angeles	--	North Coast	10
3.	East Bay	11	Clear Lake	8
4.	Sacramento	16	North Bay	3
5.	Stockton	7	Contra Costa	11
6.	Peninsula	3	Sacramento Valley	14
7.	San Jose	2	Sierra	11
8.	Fresno	--	San Joaquin Valley	4
9.	San Bernardino	1	Central Coast	3
10.	San Diego	2	South Coast	1
			Pomona	--
			Riverside	--
			North Desert	1
			South Desert	--
			North Nevada	10
			South Nevada	--

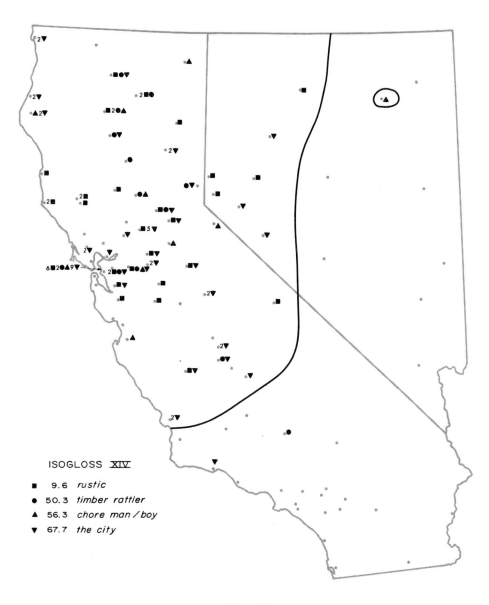

ISOGLOSS XIV

- ■ 9.6 *rustic*
- ● 50.3 *timber rattler*
- ▲ 56.3 *chore man / boy*
- ▼ 67.7 *the city*

Map 39

PATTERN XV. LOS ANGELES AND SOUTHERN CALIFORNIA

Although this group of words is very small, it substantiates a point
brought out in the first group of patterns—that is, the strong correlation
in usage between Los Angeles and the Pomona area. Also interesting is
the isogloss for the term Santa Ana (5.7) in contrast to that of chinook
(see Pattern XVI). All of the responses of Santa Ana from Northern
California referred to Southern California (see vocabulary) (maps 40
and 41).

Table 19

Pattern XV. Southern California

5.7	Santa Ana (See vocabulary discussion regarding usage in Northern California.)
9.6	batten/board'n'batten/batten board siding
15.2	sponge
25.1	bay
26.3	sanky (Los Angeles only)
54.1	acts like
	is (just) like
63.5	going together
71.6	migs

Distribution density—percentage of total possible answers on 9 items:

1.	San Francisco	1%	North Border	5%
2.	Los Angeles	26	North Coast	--
3.	East Bay	3	Clear Lake	2
4.	Sacramento	--	North Bay	--
5.	Stockton	--	Contra Costa	--
6.	Peninsula	4	Sacramento Valley	0.5
7.	San Jose	--	Sierra	3
8.	Fresno	--	San Joaquin Valley	4
9.	San Bernardino	2	Central Coast	7
10.	San Diego	20	South Coast	14
			Pomona	23
			Riverside	4
			North Desert	13
			South Desert	9
			North Nevada	2
			South Nevada	5

ISOGLOSS XV a

■ 5.7 *Santa Ana*

Map 40

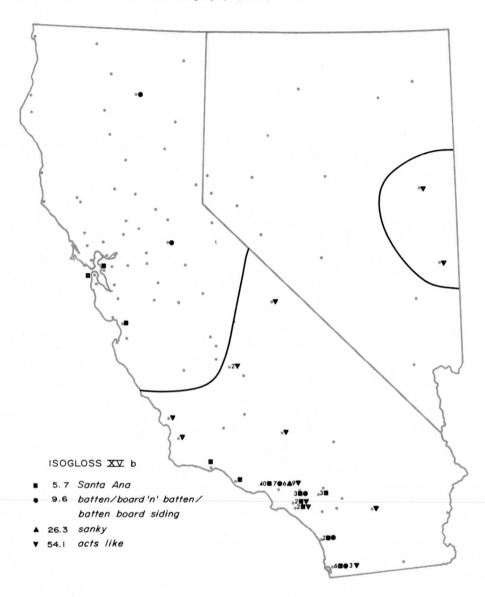

ISOGLOSS XV b

■ 5. 7 *Santa Ana*

● 9.6 *batten/board 'n' batten/*
        batten board siding

▲ 26.3 *sanky*

▼ 54.1 *acts like*

Map 41

PATTERNS XVI-XIX. NEVADA USAGE

Thus far, the emphasis has been on patterns in California, because by size, population, and urban influence, that state dominates the region. Nevada, because of its geographical proximity and historical relationship, has been considered only as one of the geographic units of the region as a whole. However, Nevada does exhibit underlying characteristics of its own that are of almost equal importance. These characteristics are illustrated in Pattern XVI, terms found only in Nevada (map 42); Patterns XVIIa and b, terms that spread through the north and central sections as far south as (a) Tonopah (91) on the west (map 43), and (b) Ely (92) on the east (map 44); Pattern XVIII, terms found only between Lovelock (84) and Las Vegas (95) (map 45).

In Pattern XVI, Nevada Terms, the first item, chinook, although it also appears in the chesterfield pattern (XIIIb), is included here because there was a high percentage of use in Nevada (over 70 percent in the north and 50 percent in the south) and because its use there was generally without qualification, whereas in California it was often qualified as "learned in Montana," etc.

Patterns XVIIa and b, XVIII, and XIX (map 46) can be interpreted as reflecting the historical trends of Nevada. As we might expect, XVII has the largest number of items, representing as it does the settlement of the state from the time of the earliest migration from the east through the north and central parts of the state, as well as the period of intense mining activities in the central portion. As in the gold rush area of California, we find the core of the Nevada vocabulary in this central area where the Comstock lode was located.

The importance of the main division of Nevada into north and south for purposes of general discussion is apparent from table 20. The decision to include Ely (92) in the southern part rests on two points: one, the fact that only twenty-one items spread from the north as far as Ely; and two, the absence of any spread to Ely among the items limited to the central area.

The table shows the relationship of these patterns to the general Patterns I-XV. The salient feature shown by the table is the close relationship of the north and central patterns to rural northern California patterns. Another interesting point is the limited number of items that are also found in XIII and XIV (tables 17 and 18). Five items which were only noted in the discussions of the general vocabulary and which did not fit any pattern or occur in large enough quantities to be placed in other categories do fit into the Nevada patterns.

Table 20

Comparison of Distribution, California and Nevada

Pattern	XVIIa 95 items	XVIIb 21 items	XVIII 30 items	XIX 77 items
S	38	7	11	42
MGD	4	6	1	5
GC	3	1	1	2
I	4	-	1	3
II	9	-	-	3
III	3	2	1	2
IV	1	1	-	1
V	1	-	-	2
VI	6	1	1	3
VII	1	1	2	5
VIII	4	-	1	-
IX	2	-	-	-
X	7	-	1	6
XI	8	3	2	4
XII	1	-	-	-
XIII	1	-	4	-
XIV	2	-	3	-
XV	-	-	1	2
Noted only	4	-	1	-

Table 21

Pattern XVI. Nevada

5.7   chinook (Also XIIIb. See vocabulary discussion.)
19.1   flipper (crutch)
58.5   [gumz]
64.2   slough (school)
71.6   potteries

Distribution density—percentage of total possible replies on 5 items)
(including <u>chinook</u>).

1.	San Francisco	4%	North Border	13%
3.	East Bay	1	Clear Lake	10
5.	Stockton	6	Contra Costa	3
			Sacramento Valley	5
			Sierra	2
			San Joaquin Valley	0.9
			Pomona	2
			North Nevada	25
			South Nevada	45

No responses from other communities.

Distribution density on 4 items (excluding <u>chinook</u>):

San Joaquin Valley	0.9
Pomona	2
North Nevada	13
South Nevada	43

No responses from other communities.

Table 22

Pattern XVIIa. North and Central Nevada to Tonopah (91)

Item:		California Pattern:
4.7	changed/changing	S
6.8	back log	S
7.6	curtains	III
7.7	bureau	GC
7.8	wardrobe (closet)	VII
9.6	clapboards	S
10.4	eaves	S
11.1	tint	X
	calcimine	Noted in vocabulary
11.8	lawn	XIV
12.8	hog pen	I
13.2	barnyard	S
15.1	rinch/rench	III, VI
16.3	hydrant (faucet)	S
16.7	burlap bag	I
	barley sack/bag	II, VI
18.8	teeterboard	S
19.3	juice harp	V
20.1	auto	X
22.5	breeches	I
24.7	bog (hole)	I
	slough	S
25.2	plain	II
25.5	meadow	S
26.7	wharf	GC
26.8	breakwater	MGD
27.6	parkway	III, VI
28.4	for	S
28.6	cur	S
30.1	Appaloosa	XI
30.3	bucked off	VIII
31.5	shoat	XI
32.2	alter	S
32.6	nicker	S
32.8	chicken house	MGD
34.1	send dog	Noted in vocabulary
34.6	near horse	S
35.2	a short distance	S
36.1	a sheaf	S
36.2	sacks per acre	Noted in vocabulary
37.8	store bread	S
38.1	snail	MGD
38.5	receipt	IV
38.7	east	S
39.6	a side	GC
40.5	scrapple	S
40.6	clabbered milk	S
40.8	smearcase	S
41.7	cook dinner/supper	S
	start dinner/supper	X
45.1	apricot [æ]	S

Item:		California Pattern:
47.2	ears of corn	XI
	fresh corn	XI
	green corn	XI
48.5	yellow hammer	XI
48.6	civet cat	XI
48.8	rodent	S
49.4	crawdad	Noted in vocabulary
	crayfish	Noted in vocabulary
50.1	shiners	XIII
53.3	family	X
54.2	brought up	S
	reared	S
55.6	scholar	S
	school boy/girl	II
55.7	paper route [rut]	S
56.1	mail carrier	MGD
56.5	coon	X
56.6	Okies (also 56.8)	XII
57.1	greaser	S
59.2	powerful	VIII
60.2	obstinate	S
60.8	was taken sick/ill	S
62.2	burial grounds	VIII
63.7	hitched	S
	wed(ded)	IX
64.1	shindig	XI
64.2	played/was truant	X
64.4	primary school	S
65.3	opera house	II, VI
	playhouse	VIII
67.7	S.F.	II, VI
69.2	kind of	S
	pretty	II
69.5	[(ɪ) jæl]	II
70.8	novelty store	XIV
	variety store	S
	Woolworth's	S
71.1	belly-bust(er)	IX
73.1	give you a lift	II, VI
73.4	lugged	S
74.1	in good spirits	S
74.4	gather	II

Table 23

Pattern XVIIb.   North and Central Nevada to Ely (92)

Item:		California Pattern:
12.8	(pig) sty	MGD
13.5	barbed wire	MGD
13.7	stone wall	S
14.6	pot	MGD
16.2	tap	S

A Word Geography of California and Nevada

Pattern XVIIb (continued)

Item:		California Pattern:
23.5	coin purse	IV, VI
25.4	meadows	S
29.5	leppy	VII, XI
	orphan	S
29.8	wild horse	S
30.7	shoes	III
32.5	bawl	GC
33.2	feeding time	MGD
33.3	come boss(ie)	S
34.5	belly band	MGD
34.8	reata	MGD
37.5	light bread	XI
38.1	cinnamon rolls	S
56.2	buckaroo	XI
57.2	nearly fell (down)	III
64.1	ball	S

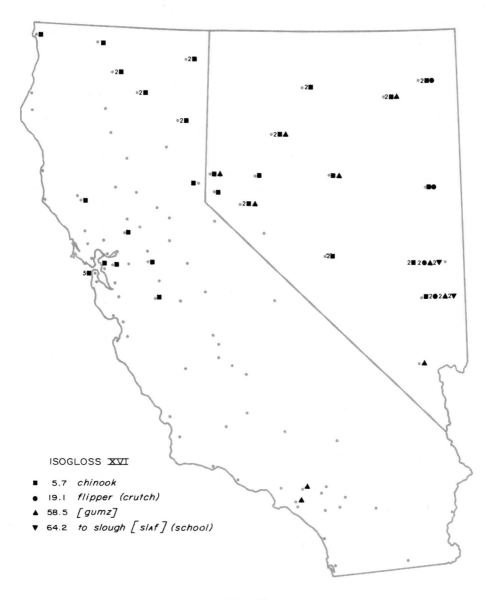

ISOGLOSS XVI

■   5.7   *chinook*
●   19.1   *flipper (crutch)*
▲   58.5   *[gumz]*
▼   64.2   *to slough [slʌf] (school)*

Map 42

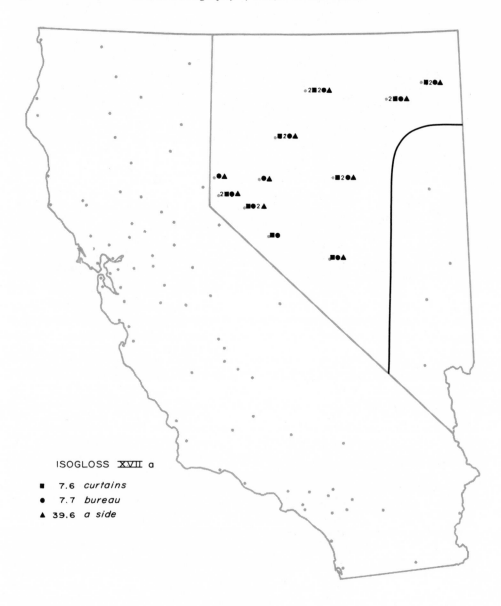

ISOGLOSS XVII a

■   7.6 *curtains*
●   7.7 *bureau*
▲ 39.6 *a side*

Map 43

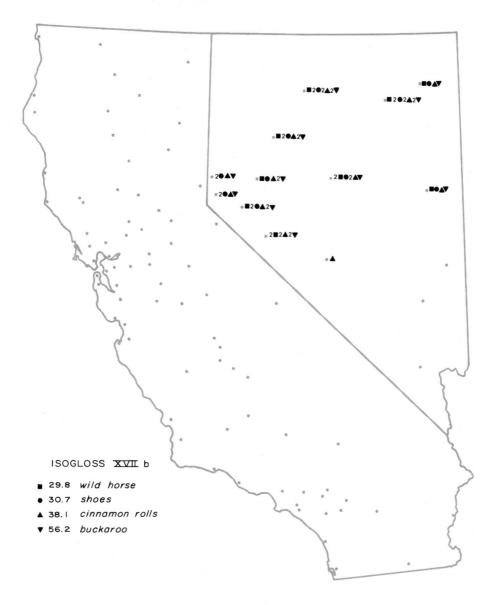

ISOGLOSS XVII b

- ■ 29.8 *wild horse*
- ● 30.7 *shoes*
- ▲ 38.1 *cinnamon rolls*
- ▼ 56.2 *buckaroo*

Map 44

Table 24

Pattern XVIII. Central Nevada

Item:		California Pattern:
8.5	does the housework/house-cleaning	XIII
12.3	granary	GC
12.6	haystack	I
18.3	sled	S
18.4	horse	III
22.8	handkerchief	VIII
23.8	bumbershoot	S
25.1	bay	XV
	inlet	VI
25.2	prairie	S
26.5	cut	XIII
27.2	macadam	MGD
30.1	paint	S
35.4	fartherest	Noted in vocabulary
38.1	bear claw	S
38.4	griddle cakes	XI
42.7	soda pop	S
	soda	X
45.8	pine nuts	XIV
46.8	cranberry beans	XIII
49.7	fishworm	XI
52.8	daddy	S
	pa	VII
56.2	vaquero	S
67.7	the city	XIV
69.4	certainly	S
69.7	huh-uh	S
70.8	notion store	XIV
73.1	see you	VII
73.5	go get	S

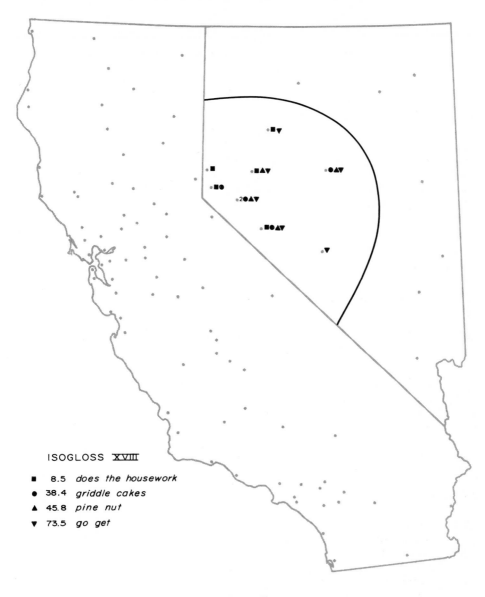

ISOGLOSS XVIII

■ 8.5 *does the housework*
● 38.4 *griddle cakes*
▲ 45.8 *pine nut*
▼ 73.5 *go get*

Map 45

Table 25

Pattern XIX. Central and South Nevada

Item:		California Pattern:
84-92:		
3.5	dawn	III
3.7	sunset	MGD
10.8	joists	S
53.1	ma	VII
54.1	is (just) like	XV
60.8	became ill	II, VI
84-93:		
3.7	dark	S
5.1	thunder and lightning	X
5.8	freeze	S
34.6	lead horse	S
35.2	a short way	V
53.2	family	X
54.1	acts like	XV
	takes after	S
55.7	[rut] of a trip	S
56.6	hillbilly	S
63.5	going with	S
69.7	uh-uh	S
74.4	cut	S
84-94:		
4.8	down-pour	MGD
5.6	letting up	S
9.8	adobes/(a)dobe blocks/	
	(a)dobe bricks/dobe	VII
11.2	toilet	S
14.3	lunch pail	GC
26.5	gap	X
30.6	hooves	S
33.3	here boss(ie)	II
35.4	the farthest	VII
48.5	flicker	X
50.5	glowworm	X
56.4	colored man	S
63.1	heave	S
63.6	broke (it) off (with him)	S
64.2	sloughed	XVI (Nevada only)
69.2	rather	S

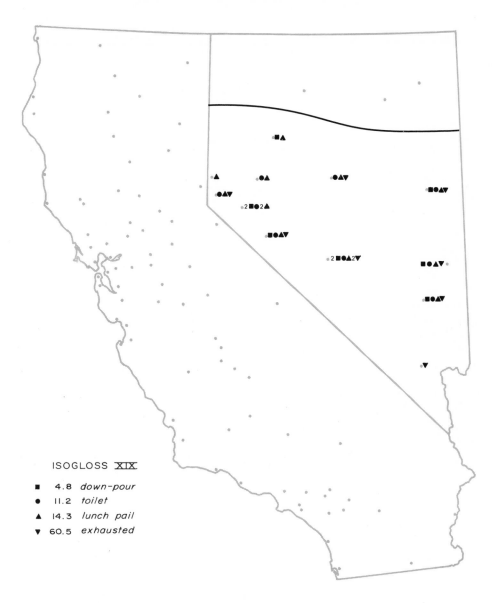

ISOGLOSS XIX

■   4.8 *down-pour*
● 11.2 *toilet*
▲ 14.3 *lunch pail*
▼ 60.5 *exhausted*

Map 46

84-95:

5.8	heavy frost	IV, VI
7.4	divan	S
7.7	dressing table	VII
8.5	tidies	I, VI
11.2	Chic Sale(s)	S
12.7	barn	II
15.4	face cloth	X
25.2	mesa	S
25.3	wasteland	S
25.6 25.7	gorge	S
25.8 26.1 26.2	wash	S (north to 83)
27.2	macadamized (road)	MGD
27.3	side road	S
27.8	at home	GC
29.2	sire	XI
29.5	dogie	S
32.6	neigh	V
34.6	wheel horse/wheeler	XI
36.2	bushel	V
38.1	coffee cake	MGD
41.6	bite (to eat)	X
41.7	fit	S
	prepare	S
49.7	earthworm	S
50.7 51.1	mud dauber	XI
54.4	illegitimate (child)	VII
56.3	hired man	S
56.4	colored people	S
56.6	farmer	S
59.3	tightwad	S
59.5	lively	S
59.6	lively	S
60.5	exhausted	S
60.8	became sick	I (95 only)
	took sick	III
61.1	caught a cold	S
62.1	died from	I
63.6	broke off/up (with him)	S
64.4	elementary school	S
65.8	wants off; wants out	S
70.8	five and ten	MGD
71.7	lag line	S

PATTERN XX. COMPOSITE OF I-XV

Pattern XX is a composite picture of Patterns I-XV, obtained by averaging the percentages of occurrence of all fifteen for each geographic area. The result emphasizes some of the general characteristics which were noted in the distribution patterns: the concentration in the Sacramento Valley and northern Nevada, and the low percentage of use along the central and south coastal areas, the north border, and southeastern Nevada (map 47).

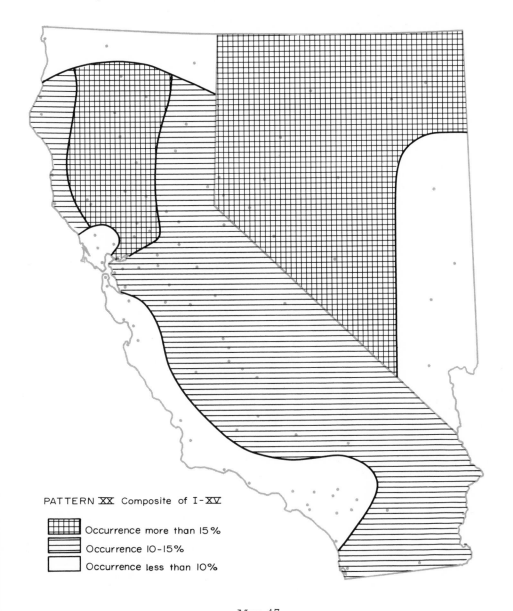

PATTERN XX Composite of I-XV

Occurrence more than 15%
Occurrence 10-15%
Occurrence less than 10%

Map 47

Table 26

Pattern XX. Composite Percentages

Urban areas:			Rural areas:	
1.	San Francisco	12.9%	North Border	5.9%
2.	Los Angeles	8.0	North Coast	13.8
3.	East Bay	14.2	Clear Lake	18.4
4.	Sacramento	15.6	North Bay	8.8
5.	Stockton	10.6	Contra Costa	14.2
6.	Peninsula	9.9	Sacramento Valley	16.2
7.	San Jose	9.2	Sierra	14.6
8.	Fresno	10.6	San Joaquin Valley	10.8
9.	San Bernardino	7.7	Central Coast	8.2
10.	San Diego	11.8	South Coast	6.8
			Pomona	6.1
			Riverside	9.0
			North Desert	12.9
			South Desert	11.8
			North Nevada	16.0
			South Nevada	9.1

SPANISH BORROWINGS

Words of Spanish origin have been divided into two groups—those used in essentially the Spanish form and those that have been Americanized through sound change, e.g., zanja > sanky; stress change, rodéo > rodeo (map 50); and morphemic change, that is, changes such as loss of endings, e.g., la reata > lariat. Altogether there are forty-nine terms, thirty-eight Spanish and eleven Americanized (tables 27 and 28).

Generally the words fall into three classes of meaning: those relating to ranching, those relating to topography, and those concerned with family and social relationships.

Of the Spanish words, the following occur in general distribution—all but the last three in every urban and rural area: patio, adobe, corral, bronco, burro, rodéo, reata, and plaza. Of the urban areas, Los Angeles, East Bay, and especially San Diego show the largest percentages of usage. In the rural areas, the distribution of mesa, arroyo, cholo, peon, and vaquero is generally limited to the central and southern regions. The remaining words occur in only scattered instances (maps 48 and 49).

Of the Americanizations, words in general distribution are lariat, lasso, and pinto. Bronc has a fairly general distribution, while bayo ['be^{I}o^{u}] bean occurs only in rural areas, and mustang generally so.

As the following distribution charts show, the Americanizations usually occur in inverse order of percentages to the Spanish words. Exceptions are San Diego, which shows the highest percentages of usage in both groups, and the North Border and North Bay areas, both of which rank low in usage (table 29).

Figures again are based on the percentage of total possible responses received in each urban area and each rural geographic area (see chapter I).

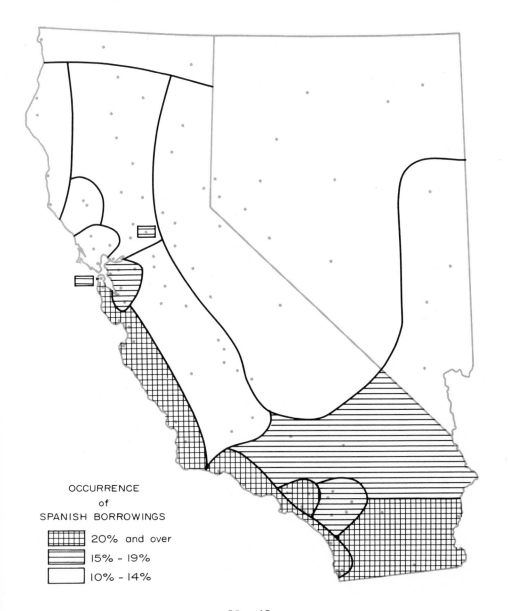

OCCURRENCE
of
SPANISH BORROWINGS

20% and over
15% - 19%
10% - 14%

Map 48

Table 27

Spanish Borrowings

		In response to:
5.7	Santa Ana	warm wind in winter
9.2	patio	porch (front)
9.3	covered patio	porch (back)
9.4	patio	court/yard
	back patio	
9.2	remada	porch (front)
9.5	remada	covered walk
9.8,	10.7 adobe(s)	earth blocks/sun dried clay
11.2	común	outhouse
	casita	
12.7	corral	cow barn
12.8	corral	pig pen
	pig corral	
	hog corral	
13.2	corral	barnyard
	feed corral	
32.8	chicken corral	chicken coop
24.7	ciénega	swamp
25.2	mesa	flat
25.4	mesa	prairie
25.2	potrero	flat
25.5	potrero	park
26.2	potrero	arroyo
25.5	hoya	park
	rincon	
25.7	arroyo	ravine
26.2	arroyo	arroyo
25.8	arroyo	creek
25.5	arroyo	park
25.6	arroyo	canyon
26.1	arroyo	gully
25.7	barranca	ravine
25.6	barranca	canyon
26.2	barranca	arroyo
26.3	barranca	a ditch/a small arroyo
26.7	embarcadero	wharf
29.2	toro	bull
29.8	bronco	unbroken horse
29.9	rodéo	
31.1	burro	small donkey
27.3	burro trail	back road
34.5	latigo	cinch
34.7	morral	nose bag

In response to:

34.8	reata	lariat
37.7	tortilla	made of corn meal
39.7	carne seco	chipped beef
46.8	frijoles	beans
49.4	langosta	crawfish
53.1	madre	mother
53.4	tata	grandfather
53.5	nana	grandmother
56.2	vaquero	cowboy
56.3	vaquero	hand
56.8	bracero	migratory worker
56.2	ranchero	cowboy
57.1	vecino peon paisano hombre cholo	Mexican
65.5	plaza	town square

(Bracketed items were counted as one term in computations.)

Table 28

Americanizations

Source:

9.8, 10.7	dobie(s)	< adobe
26.3	sanky	< zanja
29.8	bronc mustang	< bronco < mestengo
29.9	ródeo	< rodéo
30.1	pinto	< pintado
34.8	lariat (rope) lasso	< la reata < lazo
46.8	bayo(s) (bean) ['be^{I}o$^{\#}$z]	< bayo (meaning 'reddish-brown')
56.2	bronc buster buckaroo	< bronco < vaquero
57.1	pachucos/pachukes	< pechuga? (meaning 'impudence, nerve')

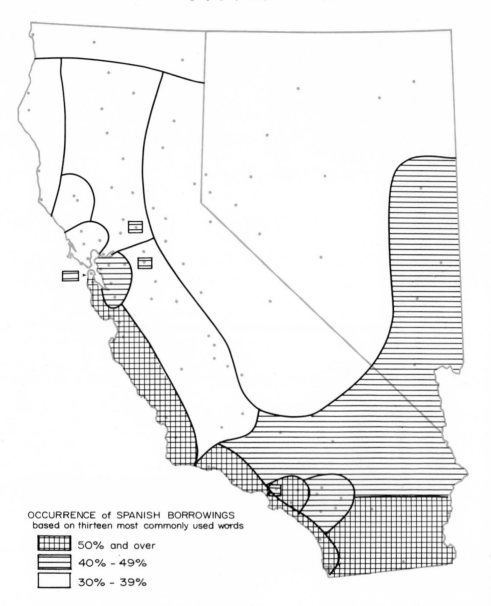

OCCURRENCE of SPANISH BORROWINGS
based on thirteen most commonly used words

50% and over

40% - 49%

30% - 39%

Map 49

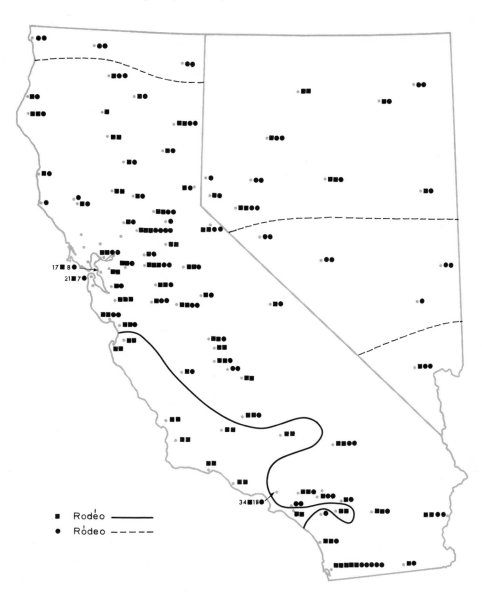

17 ■ 8 ●
21 ■ 7 ●

34 ■ 18 ●

■ Ródeo ———
● Ródeo — — — —

Map 50

Table 29

Comparisons of Tables 27 and 28 by percentages

Spanish Borrowings		Americanizations	
		Urban	
1. San Diego	25%	1. San Diego	40%
2. Los Angeles	19	2. San Jose	36
3. East Bay	16	3. Stockton	33
4. San Francisco Sacramento San Bernardino	15	4. Sacramento	32
		5. Peninsula	29
5. Stockton San Jose Fresno	14	6. East Bay Fresno	27
		7. San Bernardino	25
6. Peninsula	11	8. Los Angeles	24
		9. San Francisco	23
		Rural	
1. South Coast	25%	1. North Coast	47%
2. Pomona	22	2. Clear Lake North Nevada South Nevada	43
3. Central Coast South Desert	21	3. Sierra	38
4. Riverside	20	4. Sacramento Valley	37
5. Contra Costa	16	5. South Desert	36
6. North Desert	15	6. Contra Costa North Desert	34
7. Clear Lake San Joaquin Valley	14	7. San Joaquin Valley	30
8. Sierra North Nevada	13	8. Riverside	29
9. North Coast Sacramento Valley South Nevada	12	9. North Border South Coast	28
		10. Pomona	27
10. North Border North Bay	11	11. North Bay	25
		12. Central Coast	21

Table 30

Distribution of the Thirteen Most Commonly Used Spanish Words

Based on the following items:

9.4	patio
9.8,	10.7 adobe(s)
13.2	corral
25.2	mesa
26.2	arroyo
29.8	bronco
29.9	rodéo
31.1	burro
34.8	reata
56.2	vaquero
57.1	peon
	cholo
65.5	plaza

Urban		Rural	
1. San Diego	58%	1. South Coast	61%
2. Los Angeles	48	2. Central Coast	58
3. San Francisco East Bay	44	3. Pomona	54
		4. South Desert	51
4. Stockton San Jose	43	5. Riverside	49
5. San Bernardino	42	6. Contra Costa	47
6. Sacramento	41	7. South Nevada	45
7. Peninsula	33	8. South Desert	44
8. Fresno	30	9. San Joaquin Valley	39
		10. Clear Lake	38
		11. Sierra North Nevada	37
		12. North Coast	36
		13. Sacramento Valley	35
		14. North Border	33
		15. North Bay	32

Competition between Spanish and Americanized forms is to be seen in the distribution of the two pronunciations rodéo/ródeo (map 50). The standard method of selection of responses was changed in this case to include such responses as "some say," "they say," "used to say," etc. in order to show the areas in which the competition was apparent. About ten informants qualified ródeo with expressions of "now," "used more

recently," etc. Six qualified rodéo with "I used to say." One called ródeo
a term used in the Southwest, another stated that it came from the Midwest, and a third stated that "all Easterners" used it. On the other hand,
one Las Vegas informant volunteered that "dudes say rodéo." And a Los
Angeles informant distinguished between the two, using ródeo to mean
the show, rodéo the term used "when rounding up cattle in mountains
and fields."

Generally speaking, rodéo was more accepted in California, with heavy
concentration along the central and southern coasts from Monterey-Salinas
south—in other words, the old Spanish settlement area (cf. Patterns I-V).
On the other hand, in Nevada and along the northern border of California,
ródeo was the commonly accepted form. Except for the specific areas
mentioned, competition between the two forms is apparent in both states.

BORROWINGS OTHER THAN SPANISH

The number of words from languages other than Spanish that occurred
in the field records is comparatively small when one considers the varied
backgrounds of the early immigrants. Altogether, ten languages are represented, with a total of slightly under one hundred responses. (Indian
words are counted as one language.) Of this number, over half consists
of three Indian terms: chinook, poganip, and cayuse—words of a kind
similar to Spanish borrowings, that is, relating to nature and ranching.
The one Hawaiian term, lanai, is an innovation. The remainder are words
which had been handed down through families and are related to home
and family relationships.

The distribution of this group of words is generally limited to central
and northern California and Nevada, but again a distinction must be made
between the Indian words and the others. Only words of Indian origin are
found in Nevada; those of European origin are limited to California—mainly
San Francisco, East Bay, Los Angeles, and the Sierra and Sacramento
Valley areas (map 51).

The number of responses and any significant information for each
item are given with the list of words. Some of the words are given in
phonetic representation only, because in some instances it was difficult
to ascertain exact spellings, while in others the word given was an
obvious mispronunciation of the preceding word (table 31).

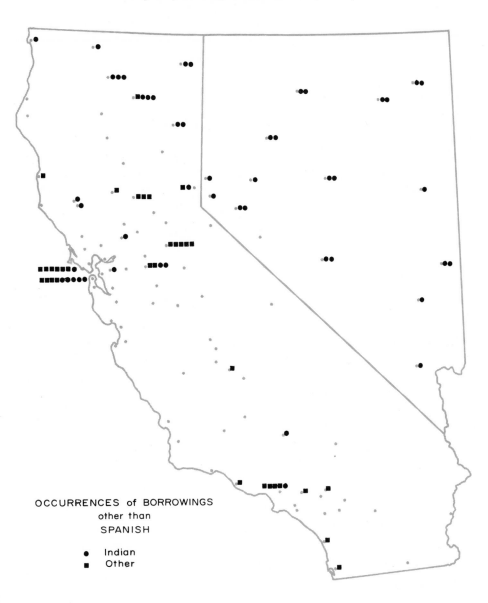

OCCURRENCES of BORROWINGS
other than
SPANISH

•   Indian
■   Other

Map 51

Table 31

Borrowings Other Than Spanish

Jewish terms:

3.2	[ˈʃaˌbᵊ/ɪs]	2 responses for 'Saturday'. Both informants Jewish.
8.2	[drɛk]	1 response for 'junk'. Jewish informant. Probably German word <u>Dreck</u>.
41.6	knosch	2 responses. "Yiddish word for wanting a small bite of food when you aren't really hungry but something looks good." Both informants Jewish.

Indian terms:

5.7	chinook	See Patterns XIII and XVI.
5.7	poganip	1 response for 'warm wind in winter'. "Used by older brother and other folks."
5.8	poganip frost	4 responses. (One informant used the [k] sound instead of the [g].) "So called by the Paiute Indians." "Very severe."
5.3	pogalip	1 response. "Very heavy foggy weather—an Indian term."
29.8	cayuse	5 responses for 'bronco'. "Mongrel horse, ill bred."
30.1	cayuse	1 response for 'pinto'. "Indian pony—not pinto."

French terms:

9.2	porte cochere	1 response for 'porch'. "If next to driveway."
9.2	[ˈpoʌpəʃɛʌ]	1 response. "For car at side of house."
9.5	porte cochere	2 responses. The mother of one informant was from Canada; the other informant was a college graduate.
9.5	[ˈpɔʌˈəˌʃɛʌ]	1 response. "Step-father spoke French occasionally."
11.2	cabinet [ˌkæbəˈneᴵ]	1 response. "Used by grandmother" for 'out-house'.
43.1	rechauffé	2 responses. "Mother used."

Italian terms:

53.4	papa grande	1 response for 'grandfather'.
53.4	nono	1 response.

Italian terms: (continued)

53.5	mama grande	1 response for 'grandmother'.
37.6	polenta	1 response "a corn meal"; informant for these four words of Italian descent.
40.5	polenta	1 response for 'scrapple'.

German terms:

53.4	grosspapa	1 response for 'grandfather', used as a child. Informant was of German parentage.
53.5	grossmutter	3 responses. (One informant was the same as above.)
52.6	frau	2 responses.
38.2	['faʃnaks]	1 response for 'doughnut'. (M. B. Emeneau, in his article "The Dialect of Lunenburg, Nova Scotia," gives [fasnak] as the name for raised doughnuts "obviously derived from the custom of making them on Shrove Tuesday, which is called [fasnakdei] from Fastnacht.")[2] The informant's husband was born in Kentucky of Pennsylvania German parents.

Hawaiian terms:

| 9.4 | lanai | 2 responses for 'patio'. "Fancy, with chairs." "Glassed in, snazzy." |
| 9.5 | lanai | 1 response for 'covered walk'. "Outdoor living room." |

Finnish terms:

| 40.8 | [fɪ^{i}lɪ^{i}ə] | 1 response for 'cottage cheese'. Informant's husband was Finnish. |

Hungarian terms:

| 40.3 | [sɨl̩ˌsə] | 1 response for 'head cheese'. |

Irish terms:

| 27.7 | [hɪn^{t}ʃtən] with a rock | 1 response for "he threw a stone!' "An Irish expression heard from father." |

[2] M. B. Emeneau, "The Dialect of Lunenburg, Nova Scotia," *Language* 11.2, June, 1935, p. 146.

Portuguese terms:

50.6   [ˈfɛɚɪbiʃ]   1 response for 'dragon fly'. "Wife's term."

Slovak terms:

40.3   [dʒɛlɪˆduᵘts/dʌts]   1 response for 'head cheese'. "Slovak name."
                                     Wife corrected to second form; her parents
                                     were Yugoslavian.

FOLK TERMS

   With each of the folk terms that follow are given the comments made
by the informants when the interviews were recorded. Since so many of
the terms occurred only once or twice, no attempt has been made to
figure out percentages; instead, the number of occurrences and the areas
in which they were found have been given (table 32).

   Professor Reed was kind enough to make available an unpublished
study, "Marble Terminology of California and Nevada: A Vocabulary and
Analysis," written by one of his assistants, Miss Claudia Buckner, which
is a detailed study of the marble terminology found in the C-N field
records and of the age groups to which the informants belonged.[3] She
reached two general conclusions:

   1. There were definite regional variations in marble usage. The
northern region covered from the north border to a line just south of
the San Francisco Bay area, Stockton, Markleeville, and Jackson, and
northeast across Nevada from Hawthorn to Wells. The southern region
lay south of a line from Los Angeles across Nevada to Pioche. In the
central area between these two sections, occurrence was lower. The
terms used here were more closely related to the north than the south.

   2. In her study of the relationship of age to marble terminology, Miss
Buckner concluded that marble playing was retaining its popularity in
rural areas but losing in urban areas.

   The marble terms included in this study are found in table 32 under
71.6.

   [3]Claudia Buckner, "Marble Terminology in California and Nevada: A Vocabulary
and Analysis," unpublished, 1967.

Table 32

Folk Terms

(Comments are taken from the field records.)

Item		Responses	Distribution
4.8	pourdown (N.)	8	Northern California

One of the informants from Mariposa in conversation: "I've seen some of those pourdowns too." The field-worker heard of another instance of this use by a native speaker. Synonyms given for the words were in noun form, e.g., cloudburst.

	gosling drownder	1	Petaluma
30.1	Appaloosa	8	Rural—see General Vocabulary and P. XI
19.1	flipper (crutch)	6	Nevada P. XVI
	Indian shooter	1	Contra Costa
	nigger shooter	11	3, 9, 10, Desert and Sierra
	toad shooter	1	6
24.4	['su^{u}gən]	2	Sierra and southern Nevada

"Not washable." "Brother used to call it. Made of denim?" See Chapter V for relation to Texas vocabulary.

27.4	kiss-me-mams	1	3
	Jocular		
	thank-you-mams	2	7, Marin

"Used by mother." "Used by grandmother."

| | ['fæ ŋkju^{++}, ma^{u}nz] | 1 | Sierra |

"Old-fashioned." This is possibly child's talk for the preceding item.

31.1	desert canary (bird)	4	Sacramento Valley and Sierra
	mountain canary	2	Sacramento Valley and Sierra
	Rocky Mountain canary	4	2, Sierra, Contra Costa, South Desert

Los Angeles informant had heard the term in Colorado.

| | Tonopah canary | 1 | Nevada |
| 50.6 | earsewer | 17 | 1, 3, 6, 7, North Bay, Contra Costa. (S.F. Bay Area) P. XIII |

"He will sew your ears up, they used to tell us." "If I wasn't a good boy."

50.6   sewing bug   2   1, Contra Costa

      Used by mother with story of sewing lips.

mouth stitcher	1	Nevada (Tonopah)
sewing needle	2	Los Angeles
knitting needle	2	Sierra and southern Nevada
needle fly	1	San Bernardino
needle bugs	1	Sierra
devil needle	2	North Coast; Benicia
devil('s) fly	1	South Desert
devil stinger	1	Benicia
stingers	1	Contra Costa
daddy-long-legs	1	East Bay

"as a child"

damsel fly	1	San Francisco

"smaller, possibly female of dragon fly"

gallinipper	1	Sacramento Valley
snake doctor	16	1, 2, 8, 9; Sacramento Valley, Clear Lake, Sierra, San Joaquin Valley, Central Coast, North Nevada
snake feeder	8	9, 10; Sacramento Valley, Sierra, Pomona, South Desert
mosquito hawk	21	2, 3, 7, 8; Sacramento Valley, Sierra, Contra Costa, San Joaquin Valley, Pomona, Riverside, South Desert, North Nevada
skeeter hawk	3	1; Coalinga
mosquito catchers	1	Sierra
flying mosquitoes	1	Sierra
gnat hawk	1	Sacramento Valley
tarantula hawk [trӕntlɔ⤙]	2	San Diego, Oceanside

"red wings" "kills tarantulas"

tommy hawks	1	Modesto
tommy tailor	1	Modesto

50.7   tarantula hawks   2   San Diego, Coalinga

The San Diego informant described it as black with yellow wings. "They kill tarantulas and lay eggs on them."

The Coalinga informant: "large, red wings, lay eggs in tarantula holes."

51.2	no-see-'em	2	North Border, Salinas

The Salinas informant: "An Oregon insect."

	no-can-see	1	Sacramento Valley
56.7	down in the dobe	1	Sacramento Valley
	out in the tules	2	Los Angeles
	out in the tule bushes	1	Los Angeles
	tule route	1	North Desert

Given by a dairyman in referring to "routes that are hard to cover."

56.5 (The responses given here for 56.5 and 56.6 were given by Negro informants.)

	boy	1	East Bay

The informant disliked all such terms of contempt.

	boot	1	Los Angeles

Jocular. "Among ourselves. May come from the color of shoes."

	members	1	Los Angeles

Jocular. "Among ourselves."

	no-good colored person	1	Los Angeles
	Sambo	2	Los Angeles and East Bay

"Not used by Jimmy Smith [informant]."

	Spook	2	Los Angeles

"I try not to use 'nigger'." Jocular. "Among ourselves."

56.6	paddy	1	Los Angeles

Applied to whites by Negroes. In general derogatory and jocular.

	peckerwood	2	Los Angeles and East Bay

Applied to whites by Negroes. In general derogatory and jocular.

57.1	Mesican	1	San Diego

Folk etymology: "Things Mexicans do are in a mess."

	[spɪkəz]	1	Central Coast

"No [spɪkədə] English."

71.6	marbles:		
	aggies	31	1, 2, 3, 10; San Joaquin Valley, Oceanside

Diminutive of <u>agates</u>

	bony	1	Sacramento Valley

Diminutive of <u>bone</u>. "Obsolete now."

	boulder purie	1	Los Angeles

   (See <u>purie</u> below)

71.6   marbles: (continued)

cat's eyes	5	1, 3, 4; Sacramento Valley, North Desert

"Like agates, only they have eyes in the marbles."
"Clear marble with dot in the center."

chalkies	12	2, 3; Central Valley, Contra Costa, Central Coast, Sierra, North Nevada
chinas/chinies	17	1, 3, 4, 10; North California and North Nevada
chinks	2	Sacramento Valley and North Nevada
chonks	1	East Bay

   "Very large."

clearies	1	San Diego
commies	1	North Nevada

"Small and brown."

comps	3	East Bay, North Coast, Sacramento Valley

"Smaller marbles." "Colored." "Glazed, tile stuff."

crocker(ies)	4	Los Angeles and San Diego

"Cheap." "Porcelainized."

dobabes/dobabies	13	10; North Coast, Contra Costa, Sacramento Valley Riverside, Desert
dobies	53	P. VI

"Clay, cheap, doughy looking."

doughie	1	Riverside

"Larger, dough-colored."

doughboys	2	East Bay, Clear Lake

"Baked clay."

glassies	68	M.G.D.
glazies	1	Sacramento Valley

"Glazed over."

imies	5	Los Angeles, San Joaquin Valley, South Coast, South Desert

"Imitation agates."

mibs (game of ____)	6	1, 2, 3; Sacramento Valley
migs	33	2, 3, 6, 9, 10; North Border, Sierra, South Coast, Pomona, Desert, North Nevada
miggies	1	Los Angeles

"Cheapest"

71.6   marbles: (continued)

megs	1	East Bay
moonies	1	Sacramento Valley
mossies	1	San Joaquin Valley

"Moss green in center."

peewees	9	1, 2, 10; Clear Lake, San Joaquin Valley, Central Coast, North Nevada

"Small," "smallest," "clay," "white like chalk, cheap."

potteries	8	San Joaquin Valley, Nevada

"Glazed brown and blue."

potters	1	Sacramento Valley

"Porcelain"

potsies	1	Sierra

"Cheap"

puries	12	1, 2, 3, 4; North Coast, Contra Costa, Sierra, San Joaquin Valley, Central Coast

"Best." "Good ones." "Solid color." "Pure white." "Like a glassie but a half moon in it—expensive." "A shooter." "Same as a taw."

realies	1	East Bay

"Real high-class glass, the best."

shooters	14	2, 3; Sacramento Valley, Sierra, San Joaquin Valley, South Coast, Riverside, North Desert, North Nevada
steelies	20	2, 3, 10; Sacramento Valley, Sierra, San Joaquin Valley, Central Coast, Riverside, Desert, Nevada

"Ball bearings." "Made of steel."

stonies	7	3, 4; Central Valley

"Glass." "Heavy lead." "Solid looking."

taws	81	P. I
tawl [tɔl]	1	San Joaquin Valley

"For shooting."

[tərɔlɚ/taroˈˈlɚ]	2	6; North Bay

"Of steel." Possibly < <u>taw</u> <u>roller</u>?

whities	2	4; North Nevada

"White." "Large—the shooter."

CHAPTER IV

THE RELATION OF CALIFORNIA-NEVADA
VOCABULARY TO THE SPEECH
OF OTHER REGIONS

Although there are many parts of the United States that have not been covered by speech surveys, five studies have been made which provide enough material to make comparison with California-Nevada speech interesting. The material in this chapter is based on the following five surveys:

Hans Kurath, A Word Geography of the Eastern United States, Ann Arbor, 1949

A. L. Davis, "A Word Atlas of the Great Lakes Region," Doctoral Dissertation, U. of Michigan, 1948, microfilm

E. Bagby Atwood, The Regional Vocabulary of Texas, Austin, Texas, 1962.

Clyde T. Hankey, "A Colorado Word Geography," Publication of the American Dialect Society No. 34, Nov., 1960.

Carroll E. Reed, "Washington Words," Publication of the American Dialect Society No. 25, April, 1956, 3-11.

In addition, the occurrences of five items on which Gordon R. Wood reports in his article, "Word Distribution in the Interior South." (Publication of the American Dialect Society No. 35, April, 1961, 1-16) are indicated in parentheses in the tables.

The questionnaire used by Hans Kurath in the eastern states formed the base for all the surveys, the others adding and deleting to fit the particular regions. Many items that are listed in the California-Nevada vocabulary are not found in the following tables because they were not included in the other questionnaires. Furthermore, the list of California-Nevada variants (table 35) pertains only to those categories included in the other surveys and is therefore not intended to be an exhaustive listing of California-Nevada regional terms. For example, the marble term dobies (71.6) may very well be a California-Nevada regional word, but since marble terms were not included in the other questionnaires, dobies does not appear as a California-Nevada term in table 35.

[118   ]

The tables have been compiled from the point of view of the California-Nevada survey—that is, tabulated according to the common occurrences of California items with the others. Words found in the other surveys but not found in California-Nevada are not given. In this respect, it should be remembered that this entire study is based generally on words used by at least 15 percent of the California-Nevada informants. Many of the words found in the other studies but not listed here may actually have occurred in California-Nevada but not in significant enough numbers to be included.

The distribution of only the Eastern vocabulary by regions has been indicated for two reasons: first, as pointed out above, the Eastern study forms the core for all subsequent surveys; second, the other vocabularies are regional in themselves and such distinctions as they make are usually of a local nature. Occasionally the frequency of use in some of the other areas is noted, but not consistently.

The following abbreviations are used:

East   Kurath's A Word Geography of the Eastern United States
                    (and similarly for Great Lakes, Colorado, Texas, and
                    Washington)

Speech areas of the East:

N	North
NM	North Midland
M	Midland
SM	South Midland
S	South
N.E.	New England
eN.E.	eastern New England, etc.
L.I.	Long Island
Met. N.Y.	Metropolitan New York
Del. Bay	Delaware Bay
I.S.	Interior South

The usual abbreviations for states and cities are used.

A summary of the California-Nevada distribution is indicated at the end of each group of words, with the same symbols as were used in chapter IV. The category numbers that are used in the complete vocabulary are repeated in this chapter again for purposes of cross-checking.

Table 33 includes terms found in California-Nevada which were found
in the East and combinations of the East and other regions; table 34
consists of terms in common with the regions other than the East; and
finally, table 35 lists variants found in California-Nevada but not elsewhere. Of the words from the Eastern list, table 33, about one-third of
the total were used in North, Midland, and South; about eight in North
and South; twenty-eight in North; six in North and North Midland; seven-
teen in North and Midland; nineteen in Midland; fifteen in Midland and
South; ten in South Midland and South; and eight in the South—the North
and Midland areas thus represented to a greater degree than the South.
In C-N distribution, a little more than a third were of general or minor
general distribution, a little less than a third scattered, and about a
fourth fitted into one or more of the patterns.

Generally speaking, words of general distribution in the East were
also general in C-N as well as the other geographies—about forty-five
items had general distribution in both the East and C-N. Of the other
words fitting into the GC-N or MGD groups, twelve were from the North;
ten each from North and Midland, and Midland and South; four from Midland; and only one from the South.

Words from regional or local areas were usually scattered in C-N
distribution or fitted in one of the patterns.

Of the words in the other surveys that were not asked in the East,
table 34, a little over a third were of general or minor general distribution in C-N, a little less than a third were scattered, and about a third
fitted into one or more of the patterns. Thus we see that the proportions
of distribution for the two tables remain much the same in California-
Nevada.

The occurrences in the patterns also show a very close relationship,
as the following table indicates:

Pattern	East	Others		Pattern	East	Others
I	4	6		IX	1	1
II	2	8		X	5	9
III	6	11		XI	10	20
IV	3	8		XII	-	-
V	3	6		XIII	1	5
VI	4	9		XIV	1	1
VII	1	13		XV	-	-
VIII	2	4		XVI	-	-

The amounts differ considerably, but the proportions remain very nearly
the same except for Patterns VII and XIII. The highest numbers (outside
of Patterns I-VII, which seem to reflect historical spread most clearly)

occur in Patterns X (Urban and Northern California) and XI (Rural). Lowest occurrences are in Patterns IX (Central Valley, Sierra and Nevada, a limited pattern in itself), XIII (San Francisco and Vicinity) and XIV (the city). From neither table do words fit into Patterns XII (Urban), XV (Southern California), and XVI (Nevada).

Of special interest is the high occurrence in Pattern VII (Central California and South) of words not on the Eastern list. Over half of these are on the Colorado list, five from Texas, and two each from Great Lakes and Washington. A glance back at the maps showing the trails of migration in chapter III will show that migrants from Colorado probably followed either the Old Spanish Trail to Salt Lake City and then the Salt Lake City-Los Angeles trail over Cajon Pass, or the trail south through Santa Fe and down the Rio Grande to the Gila Trail which the Texans used. From Southern California the trail for the migrants led naturally up the San Joaquin Valley to Central California and the gold fields. Altogether, the correlation between the patterns of chapter IV and the relation of items with other surveys seems to reflect more than mere chance as a factor of distribution.

Evidence from other parts of the country is insufficient to allow us to state unequivocally that certain words are regional or local in usage. However, on the basis of the material that we have, I would like to suggest these possibilities:

Western (from at least two of the following: Colorado, Texas, California-Nevada, and Washington):

4.8	pourdown	31.1	burro
13.2	corral	34.8	lariat
16.4	blacksnake		reata
25.2	mesa	46.8	frijoles
26.2	arroyo		pinto beans
29.5	dogie	49.6	horned toad and variants
	maverick	56.2	vaquero
29.8	bronco/bronc		buckaroo
30.1	pinto/paint	57.1	wetback
			greaser

California-Nevada:

5.1	a thunder and lightning	34.8	lass/lasso rope
9.6	rustic	46.8	bayos
16.7	barley sack		cranberry bean
26.3	sanky	57.1	cholo
29.5	leppy	64.2	sloughed school (Nevada)

Pacific: (California and Washington)

50.1	shiners
50.6	ear sewer

Generally, it can be said that the evidence that is given in chapter V corroborates the validity of the distribution patterns that were set up in chapter IV. However, we distort the picture if we do not take into consideration factors other than geographic drift that affect the distribution and use of words. One is the competition between synonyms within a region which often results in the preference of one over the others. Examples are 6.3 living room over front room and sitting room; 6.7 mantel over mantelpiece; and 16.7 gunny sack over burlap sack.

Another factor is the effect of differences in geographical location—that is, differences in climate, native flora and fauna, and topography from the region of original use of a word. For example, 51.6 sugar maple, considered a national term by Kurath, had only a 20 percent scattered occurrence in California, where the tree is not native.

A third factor is the change of meaning that a word acquires in new areas. An example here is the word 16.2 spigot (and its variant, spicket), used in California to mean the tap on a barrel. In the East, only the device on a water pipe was elicited, but spigot/spicket was common in the Midland and South for this item.

Innovation—the coinage of a new word to fit a new situation—and, conversely, obsolescence—the gradual disuse of a word that has been replaced or that represents something no longer in use—can be seen in the use of 15.2 sponge for dishcloth because of a change in the material used for the article, and 6.3 parlor, already obsolete in the East and considered old-fashioned by many in California. The latter change apparently has come about both because of competition with other words (sitting room, living room, etc.) and because of the change in social life that made a special room for entertaining company no longer necessary.

Often current events will affect word usage, possibly only temporarily in some instances. For example, the terms 56.6 Okies and Arkies were terms that became common in California during the migration of residents from Oklahoma and Arkansas to California during the dust storms of the early 1930's. A similar example is 57.1 wetbacks, for Mexicans who enter the United States illegally by wading across the Rio Grande in order to work on the farms of the Southwest and West. One term that was probably of temporary use, 50.5 glowworm, was given by several California informants because the song "Glow, Little Glowworm" was very popular at the time the interviews were made.

Finally, the balance between the urban and rural character of a region is reflected in speech. In the list of California-Nevada variants, table 35, at least ten instances of items showing a sizeable percentage of "No response" can be attributed to urban ignorance of farm terms.

Much can be conjectured about the migratory paths taken by words and the forces that affect their usage, but a real understanding will have to wait for the completion of similar studies in surrounding regions of the country.

Table 33

Terms in Common with East and Others

Terms common to all:		Distribution in East:
4.4	quarter to 11	N and S
	quarter of 11	N, NM
6.6	andirons	N, M, S
	dog irons	Parts of M, S
	handirons	Parts of M, S
6.7	mantel	N, M, S (also I.S.)
	mantelpiece	N, M, S (also I.S.)
7.6	(window) shades	Parts of N, M, S
10.4	gutters	Parts of N, M, S
13.2	barnyard	N, M, S
14.5	frying pan	N, M, S (also I.S.)
	skillet	M, part of S (also I.S.)
16.1	faucet	N, parts of M and S
16.2	spigot	M, S

(Note that this word is used with a different meaning in California.)

16.7	gunny sack	N, M (also I.S.)
	burlap sack	N, M, S (also I.S.)
17.6	singletree	M, S
18.8	teeter-totter	Parts of N, M
	seesaw	N, M, S
20.5	coal oil	M, S
	kerosene	N, parts of S
32.6	whinny	Parts of N, M
	nicker	SM, S
33.1	wishbone	N, NM
35.8	second cutting	Parts of N, M, S
36.1	sheaf	N, M, and literary
38.2	doughnut	National
40.6	clabber(ed) milk	SM, S
40.8	cottage cheese	N, M, S
	smear case	Parts of M, S
41.6	snack	Parts of M, S
	piece (-ing)	NM
	bite	Parts of N, M, S
47.2	sweet corn	General term used in Eastern Atlas
	roasting ears	Part of M; S
49.7	angleworm	Parts of N (also I.S.)
	fish(ing) worm	Parts of N, M, S (also I.S.)
51.6	sugar maple	National
63.8	shivaree	Parts of N, M

39 items: 19 GCN; 1 MGD; 13 S; Patterns: 1 II; 1 V; 1 VI; 1 X; 2 XI.

Terms in common with East:

24.6	clear	General
24.8	river	N.E.
	brook	N.E., L.I., met. N.Y.
25.1	creek (salt)	General
25.2	flat(s) (lands)	Parts of N and M
		(used in East to mean land along
		a watercourse)
39.4	pork	No. Carolina
40.5	scrapple	Phila.
51.7	(maple) orchard	Parts of N, M, S
51.8	sycamore	Ohio Valley
64.2	played hookey	N, M to Va.
	played/was truant	N, M to Va.

11 items: 2 GCN; 6 S; Patterns: 1 IV; 1 VI; 1 X; 1 XIII.

Terms in common with East and Great Lakes:

12.6	haycock	N.E., NM, parts of S
14.4	swill pail	N
17.8	hauling	General
18.4	horse	General exc. Penna.
24.4	quilt (only as <u>tied</u> in East)	N.E.
33.6	get up	General
	clucking	General
	giddy up, etc.	General
46.4	to shell (beans/peas)	General
51.7	maple grove	Parts of N, M, S
63.2	at his stomach	M, S, parts of N
71.7	belly flop	w N.E., Del. Bay
	(Some difference of meaning in parts of California)	
	belly buster	SM, parts of Va.

13 items: 4 GCN; 2 MGD; Patterns: 1 III; 1 IX; 1 XI.

Terms in common with East, Great Lakes, and Colorado:

14.1	wooden pail	N.E., parts of S
33.8	pig! pig!	N.E., M
46.4	hull (beans/peas)	M

3 items: 3 S

Terms in common with East, Great Lakes, and Texas:

12.8	(pig) pen	wN.E.
	hog pen	wN.E.
14.1	(wooden) bucket	eN.E., M, S
14.4	slop bucket	M, S
18.4	saw horse	General exc. Penna.
34.2	(come) (here) chick	General
37.5	white bread	eN.E.
	light bread	S, SM
47.1	husks	N, NM

50.5	firefly	N
	lightning bug	N
53.8	midwife	General

12 items: 7 GCN; 1 MGD; 1 S; Patterns: 1 I; 2 II; 1 VI; 2 XI.

Terms in common with East, Great Lakes, Colorado, and Washington:

7.6	curtains	N, part of S
	(window)blinds	M
10.4	eave(s) troughs	N
12.4	(hay) mow	Parts of N, NM
16.7	burlap bag	General (also I.S.)
18.3	stone boat	N exc. eN.E.
18.5	saw-buck	Pa. Ger. and Dutch
18.8	teeter	N.E. and settlement area
	teeterboard	N.E. and settlement area
53.7	baby buggy	Parts of N and M

10 items: 2 GCN; 1 MGD; 5 S; Patterns: 1 I; 1 III.

Terms in common with East, Great Lakes, and Washington:

12.4	(hay) loft	Most parts
12.6	(hay) shock	SM, S
33.3	come boss(ie)	Parts of N
36.1	bundle	All parts, esp. SM, and S
40.6	curdled milk	ePenna. and met. N.Y.
53.7	baby carriage	N.E. settlement area and S
63.2	to his stomach	N.E. settlement area

7 items: 2 GCN; 1 MGD; 2 S; Patterns: 1 V; 1 X.

Terms in common with East, Great Lakes, Texas, and Colorado:

14.2	pail (metal)	N
	bucket	eN.E., M, S
19.4	coal bucket	M, parts of S
	(coal) scuttle	Parts of N, M, S
	(coal) hod	N.E., parts of M and S
24.4	comforter	N (Calif. 45%)
	comfort	M, S (Calif. 14%)
32.4	moo	General
33.4	so boss(ie)	General
34.6	near horse	Parts of N, M
	lead horse	Parts of M
	nigh horse	N.E. and settlement area, parts of S
44.7	cling peach/clings	M (also I.S.)
	clingstone (peach)	N.E. settlement area and M (also I.S.)
46.5	lima beans	General
	butter beans	S

15 items: 6 GCN; 4 MGD; 2 S; Patterns: 2 IV; 1 VIII.

Terms in common with East, Great Lakes, Texas, and Washington:

7.8	(clothes) closet (built in)	General
9.2	porch	N, M, S
	veranda	N, M, S
14.5	frying pan	General-urban
17.5	shafts	Most parts
32.5	bawl	M
35.8	second crop	Parts of N; M; S
49.7	earthworm	Urban N; part of S (also I.S.)

8 items: 4 GCN; 1 MGD; 2 S; Patterns: 1 V.

Terms in common with East and Texas:

8.4	store room	Phila. (not elicited in all areas)
	junk room	Parts of M and S
12.8	(pig) sty	eN.E.
24.8	creek (fresh water)	General except N.E.
37.5	bread	N, NM
48.7	chipmunk	N, parts of M
	ground squirrel	M, S
54.4	bastard	General
65.8	want to get off	General

9 items: 5 GCN; 1 MGD; Patterns: 1 I; 1 III; 1 X.

Terms in common with East, Texas, and Colorado:

6.3	living room	General and urban
	front room	Most parts
	sitting room	General and rural
6.6	fire dogs	Parts of M and S
7.1	kindling	Phila. and Maryland (not elicited in N)
11.2	toilet	Parts of N.E.
	water closet (closet only in Tex.)	Parts of N and M
13.4	picket fence	N, modern M and S
13.7	stone wall	Part of N
	rock fence	SM, S
	stone fence	NM
	rock wall	No. Carolina
19.6	whetstone	N, NM, part of S
24.5	pallet	SM, S
36.8	you	General (rare in Texas)
	you-all	SM, S (most common in Texas)
39.4	salt pork	N
	side meat	NM
	sow belly	Parts of S
44.8	freestone (peach)	M, parts of N, S
50.6	dragon fly	Urban and literary
54.4	illegitimate (child)	General
65.8	want off	M
73.1	take you home	General

24 items: 8 GCN; 2 MGD; 9 S; Patterns: 2 III; 1 VI; 1 VII; 1 X; 1 XI.

Terms in common with East, Texas, and Washington:

16.5	paper bag	General
	(paper) sack	General
17.5	shavs	Most parts
38.4	pancakes	General

4 items: 2 GCN; 1 MGD; 1 S.

Terms in common with East, Texas, Colorado, and Washington

11.2	outhouse	N.E. settlement area
	privy	General
16.1 16.2	spicket	M, S (used with different meaning in California)
38.4	hot cakes	Del. Bay and Valley
	griddle cakes	eN.E., L.I. (obs. in Texas)
46.7	string beans	N, M, parts of S
	green beans	WM
48.6	skunk	N, M, parts of S
	pole cat	SM, S
50.6	mosquito hawk	S coastal
	snake doctor	SM, S

11 items: 4 GCN; 2 MGD; 1 S; Patterns: 1 III; 1 VIII; 2 XI.

Terms in common with East and Colorado:

12.2	corncrib	N, M
	crib	R.I. and parts of S
18.1	jag	Parts of M
27.8	at home	General
31.2	ram	General
	buck	N, M
34.6	wheel horse/wheeler	Va. Piedmont
38.3	raised doughnut	eN.E.
39.4	side pork	NM
54.4	catch-colt	Central N.Y. state (ketch in N.Y. and Colo.)

10 items: 4 GCN; 4 S; Patterns 1 XI; 1 XIV.

Terms in common with East and Washington:

12.5	haystack	General

1 item: 1 GCN

Terms in common with East, Colorado, and Washington:

11.2	backhouse	General
18.3	(stone) sled	M
50.6	(devil's) darning needle	Parts of N
	snake feeder	M

4 items: 3 S; Patterns: 1 XI.

Table 34

Terms in Common with Regions other than East

Terms in common with Great Lakes:

3.4	afternoon
	evening
3.7	sunset
	sundown
8.5	clean (up) (the) (house)
18.2	harrow
27.1	paved road
	concrete road/highway/pavement
	cement road
39.8	horseshoes (game)
33.2	feeding time
	chore time
41.2	sauce
43.3	vegetable garden
	garden
45.4	hull
	husk
51.3	cobweb (inside)
	spiderweb
51.4	spider('s) web (outside)
	cobweb
54.1	resembles
	looks like
54.2	brought up
60.8	got sick
	took sick
	was taken sick/ill
61.1	caught cold
	caught a cold
	took/have taken a cold

30 items: 11 GCN; 6 MGD; 9 S; Patterns: 1 III; 1 V; 1 VII; 1 X.

Terms in common with Great Lakes and Colorado:

45.3 shell (hard inner cover)

1 item: 1 GCN

Terms in common with Great Lakes and Texas:

3.5	sunrise
	sunup
5.1	thunderstorm
	electric(al) storm
7.8	wardrobe (closet)
24.2	bedspread
33.5	call to horses—by name
	by whistling
40.3	head cheese

52.8   dad
         papa
         daddy
         pa (obs. in Texas)
53.3   relatives
         relations
54.1   takes after
54.2   raised
         reared

18 items: 6 GCN; 1 MGD; 7 S; Patterns: 1 II; 1 VI; 2 VII.

Terms in common with Great Lakes and Washington:

10.5   woodshed
         toolshed
10.6   shed (built on)
         lean-to (term used in N.E. meaning a shedlike addition to a barn
                  for cows)
         woodshed
47.2   green corn

6 items: 2 GCN; 1 S; Patterns: 1 II; 1 VII; 1 XI.

Terms in common with Great Lakes, Colorado, and Washington:

16.1
16.2   tap (term used in California only with meaning of 16.2 'on a barrel')
16.3

1 item: 1 S

Terms in common with Great Lakes, Texas, and Colorado:

47.2   corn-on-the-cob (new in Texas)
73.4   lugged
         packed

3 items: 1 GCN; 1 S; Patterns: 1 IV.

Terms in common with Great Lakes, Texas, and Washington:

10.5   shed (separate) (Texas did not distinguish)
         toolhouse
17.7   doubletree
44.5   pit (cherry)
         seed
         stone
44.6   pit (peach)
         stone
         seed
         (The order of 44.5 and .6 was the same for California and
         Washington; seed was first in both for Texas.)

9 items: 3 GCN; 1 MGD; 3 S; Patterns; 1 III; 2 VI (both seed).

Terms in common with Great Lakes, Texas, Colorado, and Washington:

8.3   attic
       garret

2 items: 1 GCN; Pattern: 1 XIII.

Terms in common with Texas:

3.5   dawn
       daylight
3.6   rose
       came/come up
4.7   clearing (up)
       breaking (up)
4.8   cloudburst
       downpour
       (rain) storm (used with meaning of 5.1 in Texas)
       pourdown (less than 5% in Texas)
5.4   drought (rare in Texas)
       drouth
       dry spell
5.6   letting up
       dying down
       calming down
7.4   settee
7.7   dresser
       chest of drawers
       bureau
       chiffonier
8.1   wardrobe (movable)
8.2   junk
9.2   front porch
9.6   clapboards
14.4   garbage can
15.3   dish towel
       dish cloth
       tea towel
16.3   hydrant
19.1   slingshot (used with different meaning in Texas; some in
                 California also expressed a difference)
19.2   harmonica (used in Texas by informants of foreign language
                 background)
       mouth organ (rare in Texas)
19.7   grindstone
24.2   spread
24.3   pillow case
       (pillow) slip
24.4   quilt
25.2   plateau
       plain (-s in Texas)
       mesa
25.4   prairie (land)
       plains
       meadow(s) (land)
25.5- (combined through 26.2)
26.2   gorge
26.3   irrigation ditch
       canal

27.1	black-top
27.2	
29.5	dogie
	orphan
	maverick
29.7	stallion
	stud (horse)
29.8	bronco
	wild horse
	bronc (first in Texas)
30.1	pinto
	paint (first in Texas)
30.4	buck
	sunfishing
31.1	burro
	donkey (first in Texas)
	jackass
34.5	cinch
	belly band
34.6	off horse (in Texas, used for 'the other horse'; in California divided between left, right, and uncertain)
34.7	feed bag
	nose bag
34.8	lasso
	lariat
	reata
40.7	sour (-ed/-ing) (rare in Texas)
42.7	soft drink (rare in Texas)
	soda pop
	pop
44.2	over there (infrequent in Texas)
	over yonder (common in Texas)
46.8	pinto beans
	frijoles
	brown beans
48.6	civet cat
48.8	varmints
49.5	toad (used by educated in Texas)
	frog (used mainly by urban informants in California)
49.6	horn toad
	horned toad
	horny toad
50.7	mud dauber
51.2	chigger
51.6	maple tree
53.1	mother (new in Texas)
	mama (first in Texas)
	mom
	ma
53.2	parents
	folks
53.3	folks
53.4	grandpa
	grandfather
53.5	grandma
	grandmother
56.2	cowboy
	cowhand
	cowpuncher
	vaquero

56.4	Negro
	colored man, etc.
56.5	nigger
	coon
56.6	hick
	hillbilly
	hayseed
57.1	Mexican
	wetback
	greaser
59.3	tight
	tightwad
	a miser
59.6	spry
60.3	mad
	angry
60.5	pooped out
	worn out
60.6	lazy
61.7	sweat (past tense)
	perspired
63.5	courting (obs. in Texas)
	going with
	going steady (with)
	sparking
65.6	catty-corner(ed)
	angle (-ing) (only 2 responses in California)
	anti-godlin/goglin (only 2 responses in California)
68.7	Satan
	boogey man
68.8	ghosts
	spooks
70.8	dime store
	five and ten
	variety store

139 items: 38 GCN; 25 MGD; 51 S; Patterns: 1 I; 4 II; 2 IV; 1 V; 2 VI;
3 VII; 1 VIII; 3 X; 7 XI; 1 XIII.

Terms in common with Texas and Colorado:

6.8	back log
14.3	lunch box
15.1	rinse
	rinch/rench
25.5-	
26.2	canyon
	gully
	gulch
	arroyo
32.6	neigh
61.7	sweated
73.1	see you home
73.4	carried

12 items: 3 GCN; 2 MGD; 4 S; Patterns: 1 III; 1 V; 1 VI; 1 VII.

Terms in common with Texas and Washington:

7.4   sofa
      davenport
      couch
      lounge
      divan
38.4 flapjacks

6 items: 3 GCN; 1 MGD; 1 S; Patterns: 1 IV.

Terms in common with Texas, Colorado, and Washington:

13.2 corral (rare in Texas)
40.6 sour milk (rare in Texas)

2 items: 1 GCN; 1 MGD.

Terms in common with Colorado:

10.7 adobe
      dobe
12.2 (corn) bin
13.5 bob wire
14.3 lunch pail
      lunch bucket
16.4 blacksnake
16.6 bag (cloth)
19.6 scythestone
24.7 bog (plus compounds)
      slough
24.8 crick
25.6-
26.2 ravine
      wash
27.6 parkway
      parking
27.8 home
28.6 mongrel
      cur
33.8 suwee! (<u>soo-ee</u>! in Colorado)
36.1 shock
38.2 cake doughnut
39.6 a side (of bacon)
      a slab
56.7 (out) in the sticks (Colorado also has <u>out in the tules</u>; see C-N
                          24.7 and "Folk Terms")
64.2 ditched (school)
65.4 station
      railroad station

28 items: 6 GCN; 2 MGD; 11 S; Patterns: 1 I; 1 III; 1 VI; 5 VII; 1 VIII;
                          2 XI.

Terms in common with Washington:

9.3	(back) steps (difference not asked in Texas)
10.4	eaves
12.6	(hay) stack
18.5	saw-horse (Washington had the only questionnaire other than C-N that made the distinction of 18.4 and .5)
49.7	worm (also I.S.)
50.1	minnows
	shiners
50.6	ear sewer

8 items: 2 GCN; 1 MGD; 1 S; Patterns: 1 I; 1 VII; 2 XIII.

Table 35

California-Nevada Variants

3.7	dark
4.4	ten-forty-five
	fifteen (minutes) to
4.7	changing
4.8	heavy rain
5.1	thunder and lightning storm
	a thunder and lightning
5.4	dry year
5.6	stopping
6.3	parlor (obs. in East)
6.6	fire irons
6.8	log
	No response
7.4	chesterfield
	daybed
	loveseat
7.7	dressing table
8.1	No response
	portable wardrobe (only 2 responses)
8.2	trash
	rubbish
8.4	storage room
	No response
8.5	tidies (up)
	does the house (work)/(cleaning)
9.3	back porch
	porch
9.6	siding
	No response
	shiplap
	rustic
	board'n' batten
12.2	No response
12.6	No response
13.5	barb wire
14.4	garbage pail
	swill barrel (with _____ bucket, _____ pail)

16.2	faucet (on barrel)
16.3	faucet (in yard)
16.6	sack (cloth)
16.7	barley sack
17.5	No response (urban)
17.6	No response (urban)
17.7	No response (urban)
	singletree
18.1	No response
	half (a) load
18.3	No response
18.5	No response
19.1	flipper (crutch) (Nevada)
19.7	emery wheel
24.5	No response
24.8	stream
	slough
25.1	cove
	inlet
	bay
25.5-	
26.2	valley
26.3	sanky
27.1	cement
	concrete
27.2	asphalt
	macadam(-ized) road
	oil(ed) road
	tar/tarred road
29.4	have a calf
	to calve
	to calf
29.5	No response
	leppy
30.1	Appaloosa
30.4	rear
32.4	No response (urban)
32.5	No response (urban)
33.2	chores/do the chores/ time to do the chores
33.3	No response (urban)
	here boss(ie)
33.4	No response (urban)
33.5	No response
33.8	No response
34.6	No response (urban)
34.8	lass/lasso rope
36.1	No response
40.5	No response
40.7	turned/turning sour
42.7	soda
43.3	home garden
45.2	peanuts (goobers common in Texas)
46.8	pink beans
	No response
	cranberry beans
	bayos
47.2	ears of corn
	fresh corn
48.7	gopher

48.8   pests
        rodents
49.7   garden worm
49.8   No response
50.5   glow worm (note story on this item)
50.7   wasp
        yellow jacket
51.2   No response
        (wood) tick
51.3   web
51.4   web
51.6   No response
51.8   (Oriental) plane
52.8   father (only familiar and affectionate terms asked in Texas)
53.2   family
53.3   family
54.1   acts like
        is (just) like
56.2   ˋbuckaroo
        herdsman
56.5   No response
56.6   farmer
        country hick
        Okies
        Arkies
        rancher
57.1   cholo
        Mexican nationals
59.3   stingy
        miserly
59.6   lively
        active
60.3   peeved
        excited
        hot around/under the collar
60.5   tired (out)
        exhausted
        all in
        corked
60.6   indolent
60.8   became ill
        became sick
63.5   calling on
        going together
63.8   reception
        No response   (urban)
64.2   cut class/school
        sloughed school (Nevada)
65.4   depot
65.6   kitty corner(ed)
        diagonally
68.7   bugaboo
70.8   five and ten cent store
        five and dime (store)
        Woolworth's
        fifteen-cent store
        notion store
        novelty store
71.7   No response
73.1   help you home
        give you a lift
        give you a ride
        drive

CHAPTER V

SUMMARY

There is a maxim among dialect geographers that "every word has
its own history."[1] To this we might add that every word also tells something of the history of the people who use it. We have seen the reflection
of the migrations to California in the patterns of chapter IV and the
relation to other speech areas in chapter V. We have seen how com-
pletely the English language became the language of the region, with
only a few Spanish words surviving in their native form. And, although
there were very few examples of other foreign terms surviving through
family custom, we have found evidence of some modern borrowings
because of the proximity of the Mexican border (e.g., braceros).

In other ways the environment has influenced speech change. Climatic
conditions made the term chinook common in Nevada but little known
elsewhere; the mild temperatures of the coastal valleys precluded the
use of specific terms for snow and ice conditions and changed the term
belly-flop, meaning 'to coast lying down', to a term to be used in regard
to swimming to describe a particularly bad dive.

Similarly, the climate has decided the type of agricultural products
grown here and consequently many of the farm terms. "Out here we
don't use bushels, we use sacks per acre."

The urban influence of San Francisco was in evidence in Pattern XIII,
the chesterfield pattern. The growing influence of Los Angeles was pointed
out in the apparent flow of some terms eastward from the city and up
the San Joaquin Valley—a reflection not only of urban influence but also
of the improved lines of communication that resulted from the building
of the railroads. A related but reverse effect was the continued isolation
of parts of the central and south coastal areas because the coastal railroad line was built much later.

These and other factors that have specifically influenced California-
Nevada speech have been emphasized throughout the study. However, one
major factor stands out above all the others from the evidence that was
presented—that is, the effect of the single historical event of the gold

[1]Leonard Bloomfield, Language (New York, 1933), p. 328.

rush on this transitional area. Instead of a slow diffusion of migrants throughout the state, a sudden influx of Forty-niners followed the trails to the gold country. As a result, we found in that area a focal point as influential as the urban influence of San Francisco. I believe that this is the significance of Pattern XIV—the city pattern. And this same core underlies several of the other patterns—Northern California plus the Desert (I), Urban and Northern California (X), etc. Furthermore, with the change of flow of migration, we saw this same core beginning to show signs of becoming a relic area; it is usually in this area that we find still in use words that are considered old-fashioned or obsolete elsewhere. The gold rush, because it was important economically, concentrated the population in a relatively small area, and was of short duration, had the effect on central California of speeding up the processes of speech change.

A similar influence can be seen in the central region of Nevada, in the area of the Comstock Lode, as we noted in chapter IV in discussions about the Nevada patterns. In this area, as in the San Joaquin Valley, we found a reversal of the direction of migration when the silver mines opened; however, we lack some of the factors here, such as the urban-rural contrast, that helped to clarify the California trends. Nevertheless, the effect of the silver strike is evidenced in the concentration of items in the area between Lovelock and Tonopah.

Of the general conclusions that can be drawn from the study, three seem most important:

In relation to the eastern forms, words in general use in other parts of the country have continued in general use in this region unless, by reason of other factors, particularly strong competition occurs.

While geographic barriers have influenced the direction of the flow of speech forms, they have not prevented the spread when a strong incentive such as the gold rush is present.

And finally, the rate of the process of change has been directly affected by major changes or events in the social, political, and economic forces of the region involved (e.g., the change of government from Mexican to American; the gold rush; the building of the railroads).

The rate of migration into California continues extremely high, but now the trails lead in many directions, and urban areas are again the focal points of the region; consequently, the process of change has slowed down, and we cannot expect to find such dramatic evidence of language change again soon.

THE CALIFORNIA-NEVADA VOCABULARY

Explanation of symbols:

2.6 etc.	Category numbers used in the field records and throughout this study for purposes of cross reference.
Percentage figures	Percentage of responses based on a total of 300 informants (see chapter IV)
G.C.-N.	General California-Nevada (distribution)
M.G.D.	Minor General Distribution
S.	Scattered
P. I, etc.	Pattern I (see chapter IV)

The first entry for each item presents the term in the context in which it was to be used by the field workers.

2.6   All at once

      all at once 68% G.C.-N.

      at once 17% P. III

      (all) at one time 3% P. VIII

3.2   Saturday

      Saturday 99% G.C.-N.

3.3   good morning/until what time?/

      good morning 99% G.C.-N.

      The majority would use this term as a greeting until noon.

3.4   afternoon / the part of the day before supper; when does it begin and end?/

      afternoon 97% G.C.-N.

      Usually used from noon to 5 or 6 p.m.

      evening 16% P. VII

      Starting time varied from 3-6 p.m., the majority, 5 p.m.; end varied from dusk to midnight.

3.5 We start to work before) <u>sunrise</u>/referring to time of day/

       <u>sunrise</u> 53% M.G.D.

       <u>sun-up</u> 33% P. VI

       <u>dawn</u> 21% P. III, XIX

       <u>daylight</u> 15% S.

3.6 The sun) <u>rose</u> (at six/when did the sun rise?/

       <u>rose</u> 72% G.C.-N.

       <u>came</u> <u>up</u>/<u>come</u> <u>up</u> 18% and 6% P. II

3.7 We work until) <u>sunset</u> /referring to time of day/

       <u>sunset</u> 49% M.G.D. P. XIX

       <u>sundown</u> 48% M.G.D.

       <u>dark</u> 20% S. P. XIX

4.3 <u>half</u> <u>past</u> <u>seven</u>

       <u>seven-thirty</u> 83% G.C.-N.

       <u>half</u> <u>past</u> <u>seven</u> 48% G.C.-N.

       Seven indicated they had used this term as children but now considered it old-fashioned.

4.4 <u>quarter</u> <u>to</u> <u>eleven</u>

       <u>quarter</u> <u>to</u> <u>eleven</u> 66% G.C.-N.

       <u>ten-forty-five</u> 32% M.G.D.

       <u>quarter</u> <u>of</u> eleven 30% S.

       <u>fifteen</u> (<u>minutes</u>) <u>to</u> <u>eleven</u> 8% P. VIII, XIII

4.7 The weather is) <u>clearing</u> <u>up</u>

       <u>clearing</u> <u>up</u> 46% G.C.-N.

       <u>clearing</u> 45% G.C.-N.

       <u>changing</u>/<u>ed</u> 10% S. P. XVIIa

       <u>breaking</u> 8% P. XI

4.8 <u>heavy</u> <u>rain</u> /of short duration/

       <u>cloudburst</u> 55% G.C.-N.

       Considered more severe than a heavy rain.

       <u>down-pour</u> 36% M.G.D. P. XIX

       Serious, but not as severe as <u>cloudburst</u>.

       <u>heavy</u> <u>rain</u> 13% P. III

       (rain) <u>storm</u> 10% P. X

       <u>pour</u> <u>down</u> 3% P. XIII

5.1   thunder storm

        thunder storm 65% G.C.-N.

        electric(al) storm 20% S.

        thunder and lightning (storm) 18% P. X, XIX

        a thunder and lightning/a lightning and thunder 3% P. XIII

5.2   fog (pronunciation item)

        tule fog P. XIII

        A dense, low-lying fog. One Fresno informant said it was
        "used only in the Bay Area for valley fog."

5.4   drought /short or long?/

        drought 43% M.G.D.

        This word, together with drouth (see below), offers some
        problems in analysis because of pronunciation. The vowel
        sound is found in variations of [a, $\text{æ}_\text{ɒ}$, ɔ, a^u] and the final
        consonant sound(s) of [f, ft, t]. San Francisco and Los
        Angeles consistently used the pronunciation [$\text{dra}^\text{u}\text{t}$]. The
        other forms were scattered and formed no particular pattern
        of distribution. The distribution of drought shows much
        wider urban use (71) than drouth (37); its distribution is
        not as dense in rural areas as that of drouth but it is
        generally spread throughout the area.

        drouth 42% M.G.D. See discussion above.

        Length of time, when it was given, ranged for both terms
        from one to three months to three years, again with no
        particular pattern.

        dry spell 37% M.G.D.

        When length of time was mentioned, this term generally
        indicated a shorter length of time than drought or drouth,
        although there were a few for whom this was the only term.

        dry year 5% P. VII

5.5   The wind) blew (hard

        blew 94% G.C.-N.

5.6   The wind is) letting up

        dying down 45% (dying 3%) M.G.D.

        letting up 16% S. P. XIX

        calming down 12% P. X

        stopping 4 % P. XII

5.7   chinook /warm wind in winter; moist or dry?/
          No response 43% G.C. only
          Santa Ana 21% P. XV
          Only 4 responses in Northern California, all referring to
          Southern California.
          chinook 15% P. XIII, XVI
          In most of the responses in California, the word was
          admittedly unfamiliar or associated with other places
          such as Oregon, Alaska, Montana. Occurrence was general
          in Nevada. There is little agreement on the meaning of
          the word. Of the responses given, 4 stated the wind came
          from the south, 3 from the north and 2 from the west;
          similarly, 6 said it was a dry wind, 5 that it was moist.

5.8   We had a) frost /light or severe?/
          frost 90% G.C.-N.
          Generally referred to a light frost, although in scattered
          areas (especially in San Francisco and Nevada) it would
          be used for a light or severe frost.
          freeze 17% S. P. XIX
          Usually considered severe.
          heavy frost 16% P. IV, VI, XIX
          light frost 12% P. IV, VI
          black frost 8% P. III, VI
          Generally considered a killing frost.
          white frost 5% P. III, VI

6.1   The lake) froze over (last night
          froze over 49% G.C.-N.
          froze 49% G.C.-N.

6.2   skim ice /first thin coating of ice/
          No response 54% G.C.-N.
          (There were instances of skim ice (6) and (a) skim (of ice)
          (13) scattered from Dunsmuir to San Diego and Indio with 4
          in Nevada.)
          coating/thin coat(ing) of ice 9% P. X
          (Coat(ing) of ice only P. XIV)

6.3   living room /where guests are entertained/

   living room 87% G.C.-N.

   parlor 38% P. X

   Sixty-seven informants considered parlor an old-fashioned
   word. Seven thought of it as a formal room for entertain-
   ment only.

   front room 23% P. VI

   Eighteen informants, mostly urban, considered this term
   old-fashioned.

   sitting room 11% P. III, VI

   Eight considered this word old-fashioned.

6.4   chimney

   chimney G.C.-N.

   chim(b)ley 10% P. XI

6.5   hearth

   hearth 89% G.C.-N.

   (About 22% used the [ɚ] pronunciation.)

6.6   andirons

   andirons 74% G.C.-N.

   dog irons (9), fire dogs (6), fire irons (10), and handirons (6)
   were all found in Northern California, none farther south than
   Hanford, except for one response of dog irons in Blythe considered old-fashioned; Nevada had a response of firedogs in
   Lovelock and one of fire irons in Austin. The majority of
   those in California were in the Central Valley and Sierra.)

6.7   mantel

   mantel 88% G.C.-N.

   mantelpiece 15% S.

   (Not in the Central Valley.)

6.8   back log /in fireplace/

   log 53% M.G.D.

   back log 33% S. P. XVIIa

   No response 11%

   Generally in Southern California.

7.1   <u>kindling</u>

        <u>kindling</u> 92% G.C.-N.

7.4   <u>sofa</u> /describe/

        <u>sofa</u> 64% G.C.-N.

        Forty informants, scattered throughout the area, considered the word old-fashioned. Thirty-nine informants, 24 of whom were urban, described it as having arms and back; 12, 8 of whom were urban, said it had no arms or back; 9, all rural and all Northern California except one in Ely, Nevada, described it as having only a raised headrest.

        <u>davenport</u> 48% G.C.-N.

        There were 10 responses describing the davenport as having leather upholstery and wooden arms; the majority of these responses were from San Francisco. Of 25 responses describing it as having upholstered arms and back, the majority came from Los Angeles.

        <u>chesterfield</u> 45% P. XIII

        The majority described it as a large, heavy piece with upholstered arms and back. The one Los Angeles informant considered the term obsolete; the one Southern California rural informant from Hemet qualified his response with "some people call them."

        <u>couch</u> 43% G.C.-N.

        Forty-nine informants, half urban, described <u>couch</u> as having no arms or back; 12, over half of whom were urban, said it had arms and back; 10, again over half urban, would use the term for both kinds.

        <u>settee</u> 23% M.G.D.

        Ten informants in Northern California and 2 in Nevada considered the term old-fashioned. Twenty, all but 2 (L.A.) in Northern California and Nevada, described it as being smaller than normal. Ten, 3 in Los Angeles and the rest scattered rural responses, said it would have wooden arms and back. There were no Nevada responses in the last group.

        <u>lounge</u> 20% M.G.D.

        <u>divan</u> 15% S. P. XIX

        Seven informants would identify <u>divan</u> as one that can be made into a bed; 5, as having upholstered arms and back.

7.4 continued

day bed 6% P. X
Seven described it as flat with no arms or back; 6 said
that it could be made into a bed.
loveseat 6% P. X
This was generally considered smaller than a regular sofa
—usually for two. Note similarity of distribution between
this and day bed.

7.5   suite of furniture
set of furniture/set/furniture set 59% G.C.-N.
suite of furniture 23% M.G.D.
suite used of (hotel) rooms only. 20% P. I
Nine of the 14 responses in Nevada used suite in this sense.
furniture 16% P. II
chesterfield set 4% P. XIII
Also 2 San Francisco responses of chesterfield suite and
1 Watsonville of chesterfield suit.

7.6   window shades
shades 50% window shades 34% G.C.-N.
blinds 35% window blinds 5% G.C.-N.
curtains 24% P. III, XVIIa
Four urban responses and 3 rural regarded the term as
old-fashioned.

7.7   chest of drawers /describe/
dresser 67% G.C.-N.
The majority described dresser as having three or four
drawers and a mirror.
chest of drawers 52% G.C.-N.
Usually described as high with no mirror.
bureau 51% G.C. P. XVIIa
Thirty-two considered this word old-fashioned.
chiffonier 27% S.
The majority described chiffonier as tall; 14 considered
the word old-fashioned.
dressing table 13% P. VII, XIX
This piece was generally considered to be made especially
for women, low, sometimes with kneehole and drawers on
each side, with mirror.

7.7 cont.   looking glass/glass 10% (Not included in the work sheet.)
P. II, VI
This item occurred incidentally with a decidedly rural
pattern.

7.8   clothes closet /built in/
    closet 63% G.C.-N.
    clothes closet 49% G.C.-N.
    wardrobe/wardrobe closet 13% P. VII, XVIIa
    Fifteen of the 19 urban responses were in Los Angeles.

8.1   wardrobe /movable/
    wardrobe 64% G.C.-N.
    No response 11%
    There seemed to be some confusion between this and the
last item in 7.8. The confusion probably is the result of a
new meaning—built-in closet with sliding doors—replacing
the old—a movable closet. There were 5 responses of
portable wardrobe; 4 of these gave wardrobe for 7.8.

8.2   junk /old, worthless furniture and implements/
    junk 92% G.C.-N.
    Generally considered to have some small value.
    trash 35% M.G.D.
    Over half of the responses were urban. Trash generally
indicated material of little or no value.
    rubbish 24% P. VII
    This word was used to indicate material of least value, to
be thrown away or burned.

8.3   attic
    attic 97% G.C.-N.
    garret 7% P. XIII

8.4   store room
    store room 57% G.C.-N.
    storage room 11% P. I
    junk room 9% P. X
    No response 9%
    Thirteen of the responses were from urban Southern
California.

8.5   She) cleans up (every morning
    cleans, cleans up, cleans house, cleans the house 85% G.C.-N.
    tidies (up) 12% P. I, VI
    does the housework, does the (house) cleaning 10% P. XIII,
    XVIII

8.6   The broom is) behind (the door
    behind 70% G.C.-N.
    back of 20% S.

8.7   Who does) the laundry
    the laundry 52% G.C.-N.
    Ten informants would use this word to mean commercial
    laundry only. Nine used it to mean both washing and ironing.
    washing 50% G.C.-N.
    Seven (6 in San Francisco and 1 in Anaheim) would mean
    the ironing was included, 17 would not.
    washing and ironing 25% S.

8.8   basement /describe/
    basement 85% G.C.-N.
    Thirty-seven said a basement would be finished, 12 said
    unfinished, and 8 that it would be either way.
    cellar 61% G.C.-N.
    In contrast to basement, cellar was considered unfinished
    by 44 informants, finished by only 7. In addition, 26 thought
    of it as an old-fashioned word and 21 as a place used only
    for storing food. Of the last group, all but 2 were from
    rural areas.

9.1   shut the door
    shut 80% G.C.-N.
    Nine considered this word less polite than close, 7 as more
    emphatic; 8 would use it as a command, 4 when in a hurry,
    and 3 when angry.
    close 75% G.C.-N.
    Seventeen considered this the more polite of the two words.

9.2   <u>porch</u> /at front door; describe/
           <u>porch</u> 84% G.C.-N.
           Of those who gave descriptions, 23 said the porch would
           have a roof; 11 would use the word as a general term to
           cover any type of construction, 8 described it as large,
           while 7, all in San Francisco, called it small.
           <u>front porch</u> 28% S.
           This term was not given in San Francisco.
           <u>veranda</u> 9% S.
           Over half of the total responses were from San Francisco,
           where 10 described it as large, 3 small, 8 covered, and 4
           with a railing. In other areas, 4 said it would be large.
           Three considered the term old-fashioned. One Monterey
           informant used it especially for the second story of a house.

9.3   <u>porch</u> /at back door; describe/
           <u>back porch</u> 65% G.C.-N.
           Not enough descriptions were given to draw any general
           conclusions. There were only 2 responses from San Fran-
           cisco.
           <u>porch</u> 34% S.
           <u>Porch</u> was much more common in San Francisco (17) than
           <u>back porch</u> (2). Note the difference in the state as a whole,
           where <u>porch</u> was generally used to designate the front porch,
           and <u>back porch</u> identified the opposite.
           <u>step(s)</u> / <u>back steps</u> 9% P. VII

9.4   <u>patio</u>
           <u>patio</u> 89% G.C.-N.

9.5   <u>covered walk</u>
           <u>No response</u> 26% S.
           <u>breezeway</u> 23% S.
           <u>canopy</u> 13% P. I, VI

9.6   <u>clapboards</u> /on side of house/
               <u>siding</u> 34% M.G.D.
               <u>clapboards</u> 19% S. P. XVIIa
               <u>No response</u> 17% S.
               <u>shiplap</u> 14% P. I
               <u>rustic</u> 13% P. XIV
               <u>batten/board</u> 'n' <u>battens</u> 4% P. XV

9.7   shakes /boards split or riven as a substitute for shingles/
            shakes 51% G.C.-N.
            No response 15% S.

9.8   adobes /earth blocks used in building; mixed with straw?/
            adobe(s) 25% P. VII, XIX
            (See also 10.7. Some field workers combined these items.)
            (a)dobe bricks 17% P. VII, XIX
            (Adobe blocks, 8%, had a similar distribution—Salinas to
            Banning.)
            dobe 16% P. VII, XIX

10.1   I) drove in (a nail
            drove 95% G.C.-N.

10.2   I) have driven (many a nail
            have driven 79% G.C.-N.
            drove 18% P. II

10.4   gutters /built in or suspended?/
            gutters 59% G.C.-N.
            Twenty-one said that gutters would be suspended, 10 that
            they would be built in.
            eave(s) troughs 12% S. P. XVIIa
            There was a great deal of variation in the pronunciation of
            this item. Eave and eaves were about equally divided in
            usage. The following variations of troughs were found:
            [trɔft, trɔəs, trɔ̌z, traθz]. Six mentioned that they were
            suspended.
            eaves 11% S.
            Five suspended; 1 each built in, attached (?), either.

10.5   shed /separate; for wood, tools, etc./
            woodshed 50% G.C.-N.
            shed 37% S.
            tool shed 26% S.
            toolhouse 12% S.

10.6   shed /built on; for wood, tools, etc./
            lean-to 31% G.C.-N.
            shed 25% P. VII
            woodshed 21% P. II

10.7   adobe /sun-dried clay for building/ (see 9.8)
               adobe 53% (cf. 9.8) P. VII
               dobe 34% P. VII

10.8   beams /roof supports/
               rafters 71% G.C.-N.
               Rafters were described as slanting by 102, as horizontal
               by 5, and either way by 7.
               beams 58% G.C.-N.
               Fifty-two described beams as horizontal, 10 as slanting,
               and 36 as either way.
               joists 31% S. P. XIX
               Twenty-three responses of horizontal, 11 of slanting, and
               4 of vertical.

11.1   They will) tint (the walls /interior only?/
               paint 97% G.C.-N.
               Seven would use paint for interior or outside; 18 made the
               distinction that paint has an oil base.
               tint 37% P. X, XVIIa
               Thirty percent described this as having a water base; 7%
               would use the word to mean color only. Seven urban
               informants considered the word old-fashioned.
               (Calcimine, 5%, had a distribution somewhat similar.)

11.2   out-house /separate structure; usual and jocular words/
               out-house 63% G.C.-N.
               privy 33% M.G.D.
               Chic Sale(s) 25% S. P. XIX
               Twenty-nine gave this as a specifically jocular term.
               toilet 21% S. P. XIX
               backhouse 20% S.
               water closet 8% P. X

11.4   I) haven't done (it
               haven't done 79% G.C.-N.

11.5   He) doesn't (care
               doesn't 63% G.C.-N.
               don't 42% G.C.-N.

11.6   I) <u>have</u> <u>been</u> <u>thinking</u> (about it
            <u>have</u> <u>been</u> <u>thinking</u> 53% (includes contraction) M.G.D.
            <u>been</u> <u>thinking</u> 34% S.

11.8   <u>yard</u> /area surrounding a house in town/
            <u>yard</u> 89% G.C.-N.
            <u>garden</u> 16% P. I
            Usually considered to be the landscaped or cultivated part.
            <u>lot</u> 14% P. X
            Four mentioned that it referred to the ground only.
            <u>lawn</u> 5% P. XIV, XVIIa

12.1   <u>barn</u> /what is it used for? include compounds/
            <u>barn</u> 99% G.C.-N.
            Thirty-five would use for animals, feed, and equipment;
            24 for animals and feed only; 7 for feed and equipment
            only.
            Compounds given: (Urban areas 3, 4, 8) <u>haybarn</u> (32
            responses); <u>horse</u> <u>barn</u> (25); <u>cow</u> <u>barn</u> (22); <u>dairy</u> <u>barn</u> (17);
            <u>cattle</u> <u>barn</u> (7). The last 2 were limited in California to the
            north; there were no instances of <u>cattle</u> <u>barn</u> in Nevada. The
            following compounds occurred four times or less: <u>feed</u> <u>barn</u>,
            <u>livestock</u> <u>barn</u>, <u>milk</u> <u>barn</u>, <u>pig</u> <u>barn</u>, <u>storage</u> <u>barn</u>, <u>stock</u> <u>barn</u>,
            <u>sheep</u> <u>barn</u>. There were 2 urban responses in this group,
            both East Bay.

12.2   <u>corn</u> <u>crib</u> /building for storing corn/
            <u>corn</u> <u>crib</u> 44% G.C.-N.
            (<u>corn</u>) <u>bin</u> 15% P. VII
            No response 11%
            <u>crib</u> 9% S.

12.3   <u>granary</u>
            <u>granary</u> 73% G.C. P. XVIII

12.4   <u>hayloft</u> /upper part of barn; describe/
            <u>loft</u> 56% G.C.-N.
            <u>hayloft</u> 51% G.C.-N.
            (<u>hay</u>)<u>mow</u> 12% S.

12.5   hay stack /observe shape and size; out of doors or in barn?/
            hay stack 74% G.C.-N.
            No particular pattern on size and shape; 59 mentioned that
            it would be out of doors.
            stack (_____ of hay) 29% M.G.D.

12.6   haycock /in field/
            shock (hay _____; _____ of hay) 38% M.G.D.
            No response 22% S.
            (hay) stack 18% P. I, XVIII
            haycock / cocks of hay 15% S.

12.7   cow-barn /shelter for cows/
            (cow) shed 33% M.G.D.
            cow-barn 32% S.
            barn 28% P. II, XIX
            Those using shed generally described it as being open on
            at least one side; those using cow-barn or barn were more
            apt to describe it as a closed structure.

12.8   pig pen /shelter and enclosure for hogs and pigs/
            (pig) pen 64% G.C.-N.
            (pig) sty 35% M.G.D. XVIIb
            hog pen 12% P. I, XVIIa

13.2   barnyard /where stock is kept or fed/
            corral 73% G.C.-N.
            barnyard 24% S. P. XVIIa
            Corral was generally described as being enclosed with a
            fence; there was less agreement on barnyard; some regarded
            it as open, some closed.

13.3   farm /small country place where crops are grown/
            farm 71% G.C.-N.
            ranch 56% G.C.-N.

13.4   picket fence
            picket fence 95% G.C.-N.

13.5   barbed wire fence

        barb wire fence 53% G.C.-N.

        barbed wire fence 29% M.G.D. P. XVIIb

        bob wire fence 22% S.

13.7   stone wall /of loose stones/

        rock fence 34% M.G.D.

        stone wall 29% S. P. XVIIb

        stone fence 22% S.

        rock wall 14% P. III

13.8   china /china egg

        china 82% G.C.-N.

        glass egg 35% M.G.D.

        china egg 22% S.

        nest(ing) egg 17% S.

14.1   bucket /wooden vessel/

        bucket 70% G.C.-N.

        wood(en) bucket 27% P. II

        (Note: wooden pail (6%) has similar distribution except for

        2 responses in Los Angeles and Oceanside.)

14.2   pail /large open tin vessel for water, milk/

        pail 54% M.G.D.

        bucket 54% (Plus compounds of galvanized-, iron-, metal-,

        milk-, tin-, 63%)

14.3   lunch pail /small tin container for carrying lunch/

        lunch pail 47% G.C. P. XIX

        lunch box 42% M.G.D.

        lunch bucket 30% M.G.D.

14.4   garbage pail

        garbage can 76% G.C.-N.

        garbage pail 32% S.

        The majority described garbage can as a large container

        placed outside the house. Garbage pail was used to mean

        a small container inside the house generally. Four informants

        qualified the latter term as used in the city only.

14.4 cont.

slop bucket 16% P. II, VI, XI
A rural term used for garbage for hogs. (Only 9 urban responses.)
swill barrel / bucket / pail 12% P. XI

14.5　frying pan /flat or round? iron or sheet metal? legs?/
frying pan 89% G.C.-N.
skillet 56% G.C.-N.
These terms were synonymous; both were described by the majority as flat, no legs, and material divided between cast iron and other metals.
The term spider was given in 20 responses as having been heard from older people; it was considered old-fashioned now.

14.6　kettle /heavy iron vessel with large opening/
kettle 56% G.C.-N.
pot 29% M.G.D. P. XVIIb
tea kettle 24% Only use for kettle M.G.D.
Dutch oven 10% P. VII

14.7　vase
vase 98% G.C.-N.
The [ei] vowel was generally accepted; 36 instances of the [a] vowel were given, half of them qualified as meaning a more expensive article (over $1, $4, or $5) and 20 using the term jocularly.

14.8　I must) wash (the dishes
wash 95% G.C.-N.

15.1　She) rinses (the dishes
rinses 93% G.C.-N.
rinches / renches 13% P. III, VI, XVIIa

15.2　dish rag /for washing dishes/
dish rag 70% G.C.-N.
dish cloth 42% M.G.D.
sponge 4% Innovation P. XV
Seven informants said this was the term they used "now."

15.3   dish towel /for wiping dishes/
                dish towel 76% G.C.-N.
                dish cloth 20% S.
                tea towel 18% S.

15.4   wash cloth /for face/
                wash cloth 57% G.C.-N.
                wash rag 51% G.C.-N.
                face cloth 10% P. X, XIX
                face rag 4% P. X

15.5   bath towel
                bath towel 86% G.C.-N.
                towel 18% S.

15.6   barrel /for flour, meal/
                barrel 98% G.C.-N.

16.1   faucet /on water pipe at kitchen sink/
                faucet 96% G.C.-N.

16.2   spigot /on barrel/
                spigot 42% M.G.D.
                spicket 34% M.G.D.
                faucet 17% S.
                tap 15% S. P. XVIIb

16.3   faucet /on water pipe in yard/
                faucet 83% G.C.-N.
                hydrant 16% S. P. XVIIa

16.4   whip /for driving horses/
                whip G.C.-N.
                blacksnake 3% P. VII, XI

16.5   paper bag /made of paper/
                paper bag 72% G.C.-N.
                bag 34% S.
                sack / paper sack 30% S.

16.6   <u>sack</u> /made of cloth/
          <u>sack</u> 77% G.C.-N.
          <u>bag</u> 17% S.

16.7   <u>burlap</u> bag
          <u>gunny</u> <u>sack</u> 56% G.C.-N.
          <u>burlap</u> <u>sack</u> 27% P. II, VI
          <u>burlap</u> <u>bag</u> 17% P. I, XVIIa
          <u>barley</u> <u>sack</u> / <u>bag</u> 13% P. II, VI, XVIIa

16.8   <u>tin</u> <u>can</u>
          <u>can</u> 61% M.G.D.
          <u>tin</u> <u>can</u> 55% M.G.D.
          <u>tin</u>: made of __ 24% S.
              container 14% S.
          Ten used <u>tin</u> specifically for "container for sardines."

17.1   <u>clothes</u> <u>basket</u>
          <u>clothes</u> <u>basket</u> 82% G.C.-N.
          (<u>clothes</u>) <u>hamper</u> 8% P. VII

17.3   <u>cork</u> /made of cork/
          <u>cork</u> 95% G.C.-N.

17.4   <u>stopper</u> /made of glass/
          (<u>glass</u>) <u>stopper</u> 86% G.C.-N.
          (Six percent used <u>glass</u> <u>stopper</u>.)

17.5   <u>shafts</u> /of a buggy/
          <u>shafts</u> 40% M.G.D.
          <u>shavs</u> 37% M.G.D.
          No response 14%
          Three-fourths of those with <u>no</u> <u>response</u> were urban.

17.6   <u>whiffletree</u> /on a one-horse rig/
          <u>singletree</u> 57% G.C.-N.
          <u>No</u> <u>response</u> 23%
          Seventy-nine percent of those with <u>no</u> <u>response</u> were urban.

17.7 <u>doubletree</u> /on a two-horse rig/

      <u>doubletree</u> 50% G.C.-N.

      <u>No response</u> 31%

      Seventy-four percent of those with <u>no response</u> were urban.

      <u>singletree</u> 4% P. I

17.8 He was) <u>hauling</u> (wood in his wagon

      <u>hauling</u> 88% G.C.-N.

18.1 <u>jag</u> /partial load on a wagon/

      <u>No response</u> 44% M.G.D.

      <u>jag</u> 30% S.

      <u>half</u> (<u>a</u>) <u>load</u> 14% P. I

      <u>small load</u> 6% P. IX

18.2 <u>harrow</u>

      <u>harrow</u> 81% G.C.-N.

      (Of 27 <u>no response</u>, 25 were urban, 1 Taft, 1 Carson City.)

18.3 <u>stone boat</u> /for transporting stones from fields/

      <u>No response</u> 42% S.

      <u>sled</u> 28% S. P. XVIII

      <u>stone boat</u> 15% S.

18.4 <u>saw-horse</u> /for holding boards for sawing/

      <u>saw-horse</u> 82% G.C.-N.

      <u>horse</u> 19% P. III, XVIII

18.5 <u>saw-buck</u> /for holding firewood for sawing/

      <u>saw-horse</u> 34% M.G.D.

      <u>saw-buck</u> 33% M.G.D.

      <u>No response</u> 18% S.

18.8 <u>seesaw</u>

      <u>teeter-totter</u> 61% G.C.-N.

      <u>seesaw</u> 38% S.

      <u>teeter</u> 16% S.

      <u>teeterboard</u> 10% S. P. XVIIa

19.1   slingshot /boy's weapon made of forked stick with rubber strips/
               slingshot 98% G.C.-N.
               flipper(crutch) 2% P. XVI

19.2   mouth organ /blown/
               harmonica 94% G.C.-N.
               mouth organ 21% S.

19.3   Jew's harp /held between the teeth and picked/
               Jew's harp 60% G.C.-N.
               juice harp 19% P. V, XVIIa

19.4   coal scuttle
               coal bucket 46% G.C.-N.
               (coal) scuttle 34% P. V
               (coal) hod 10% P. V

19.5   wheelbarrow
               wheelbarrow 96% G.C.-N.
               wheelbarrel 3% P. XIV
               One in San Francisco noted "not wheelbarrel."

19.6   whetstone /portable, for sharpening scythe/
               whetstone 68% G.C.-N.
               scythe stone 3% P. VIII

19.7   grindstone /revolves/
               grindstone 82% G.C.-N.
               emery wheel 11% P. II, VI

19.8   flat iron /non-electric/
               flat iron 62% G.C.-N.
               sad iron 21% S.
               iron 16% S.

20.1   a brand new) car
               car 84% G.C.-N.
               automobile 56% G.C.-N.
               auto 12% P. X, XVIIa
               machine 8% P. X

20.1 cont.

> Three considered the word old-fashioned.
>
> jalopy 5% P. XII
>
> Slang. (Also 6 responses of "old wreck" in Los Angeles.)

20.5 kerosene

> coal oil 75% G.C.-N.
>
> kerosene 74% G.C.-N.
>
> Eight said that kerosene was a newer term; 21 that coal oil
> was old-fashioned. One informant from Eureka said that
> kerosene was a Standard Oil Company trade name.

20.6 nut /on a bolt/

> nut 96% G.C.-N.

21.1 I am going (today /Is the auxiliary verb omitted?/

> I am going 96% G.C.-N.

21.2 I am not (going to

> I am not 90% G.C.-N.
>
> ain't 10% S.

21.4 here are your clothes! /mother to child, etc./

> here's / there's your clothes 47% M.G.D.
>
> here / there are your clothes 46% M.G.D.

21.5 I have) brought (your coat

> brought 95% G.C.-N.

21.6 I'm right,) am I not?

> am I not 54% M.G.D.
>
> ain't I 27% S.
>
> aren't I 19% S.

21.7 No,) it wasn't I

> it wasn't me 67% G.C.-N.
>
> it wasn't I 34% M.G.D.

22.5　trousers

> pants 83% G.C.-N.
>
> trousers 70% G.C.-N.
>
> slacks 48% M.G.D.
>
> breeches 7% P. I, XVIIa
>
> overalls 6% P. XI
>
> jeans 3% P. XI
>
> As part of a suit: trousers, 39; pants, 44. Eighteen considered trousers synonymous with pants; 14 pants synonymous with trousers. Slacks were generally considered to be for sportswear only.

22.6　His coat) fitted (me

> fit 79% G.C.-N.
>
> fitted 21% S.

22.8　head scarf /tied under chin/

> scarf 76% G.C.-N.
>
> bandanna 26% S.
>
> handkerchief 8% P. VIII
>
> (There were 23 responses of fascinator, many of which were suggested. Fourteen of them qualified the word as old-fashioned.)

23.2　They) knitted (sweaters

> knit 52% G.C.-N.
>
> knitted 51% M.G.D.

23.3　The collar) shrank

> shrunk 79% G.C.-N.
>
> shrank 23% S.

23.4　It) has shrunk

> has shrunk 87% G.C.-N.

23.5　purse

> purse 88% G.C.-N.
>
> handbag 48% G.C.-N.
>
> bag 24% S.
>
> coin purse 19% P. IV, VI, XVIIb
>
> pocketbook 16% S.

23.5 cont.

Forty described <u>purse</u> as small, 6 as large and 8 as either. Eleven used it as a general term; 6 as a synonym for <u>handbag</u>, and 4 considered it an old-fashioned term. <u>Handbag</u> was described as large by 17; 6 used it as a general term, 4 as synonymous with <u>purse</u>, and 2 considered it old-fashioned. <u>Bag</u> was described as large by 11, a general term by 2 and synonymous with <u>purse</u> by 1.

Forty-two described <u>coin purse</u> as being used for change only, and 19 as small.

<u>Pocketbook</u> was described as small (7), for coins (4), old-fashioned (3), and general term (2).

23.6 <u>billfold</u>

<u>wallet</u> 76% G.C.-N.
<u>billfold</u> 30% M.G.D.

23.8 an old) <u>umbrella</u>

<u>umbrella</u> 100%
<u>parasol</u> 18% P. XI
Twenty-three said it was used only as a sunshade, 9 that it was old-fashioned.
<u>bumbershoot</u> 17% S. P. XVIII
Used as a jocular term by 28, by 11 as an old-fashioned one.

24.1 <u>rubbers</u>

<u>rubbers</u> 86% G.C.-N.
<u>galoshes</u> 70% G.C.-N.
<u>overshoes</u> 39% M.G.D.
<u>rubbers</u>: low, 169; worn by men, 47; by women, 5; by both, 50; by child, 5.
<u>galoshes</u>: high, 132; by women, 99; by men and women, 14; with fasteners, 20; synonymous with <u>overshoes</u>, 13.
<u>overshoes</u>: high, 54; low, 9; worn by men, 19; by men and women, 13; fasteners, 14; heavy (for snow, etc.), 17; synonymous with <u>rubbers</u>, 8, with <u>galoshes</u>, 13.

24.2 <u>bed-spread</u>

<u>bed-spread</u> 67% G.C.-N.
<u>spread</u> 46% M.G.D.

24.3 pillow case
> pillow case 69% G.C.-N.
> (pillow) slip 49% M.G.D.

24.4 quilt /tied or quilted? washable?/
> quilt 81% G.C.-N.
> comfort(er) 59% G.C.-N.
> Comforter was used by 135, comfort by 43; no particular
> pattern was discernible.
> Quilt was described as tied (48), quilted (37), both/either
> (46); washable (49), not washable (21); sewed (37); thin (13);
> filled (32), 10 of which specified cotton, 3 down; pieced (26).
> Comfort(er) was described as tied (51), quilted (21), either
> (15); sewed (14); filled (59), 10 specifying wool, 12 cotton,
> and 22 down or feathers; washable (27), not washable (34);
> heavy (12), and thick (8).

24.5 pallet /bed on floor/
> No response 61% G.C.-N.
> pallet 16% P. XI

24.6 It goes) clear (across
> clear 81% G.C.-N.

24.7 swamp /inland/
> swamp 71% G.C.-N.
> marsh 46% M.G.D.
> slough 17% S. P. XVIIa
> bog / bog hole / bogland / boggy (mire) 12% P. I, XVIIa
> tules / tule land / tule swamp 5% P. XIV
> Descriptions:
> swamp: With trees (29), no trees (19), optional (10); with
> water (23), running water (4), standing water (5); grass (13);
> reeds (20); mud(dy) (6).
> marsh: No trees (20), with trees (3), optional (2); with water
> (18), standing water (3), salt water (2); grass (17); reeds (13);
> mud(dy) (7).
> slough: With water (8), standing water (4), running water (2);
> backwater (6); reeds (4); grass (3); for drainage (3).

24.8   <u>creek</u> /small fresh water stream/

<u>stream</u> 71% G.C.-N.

<u>creek</u> 59% G.C.-N.

<u>crick</u> 39% G.C.-N.

<u>river</u> 29% S.

<u>brook</u> 23% S.

<u>slough</u> 4% P. XIV

<u>Stream</u> was considered a general term by 24; as small by 34, medium by 51, and large by 29; synonymous with <u>creek</u>/ <u>crick</u> by eighteen.

<u>Creek</u> was used as a general term by only 2; as small by 59, medium by 25 and large by 11.

<u>River</u> was used as a general term by 4; as small by only 2, medium by 19, and large by 40.

Although <u>slough</u> was given as a response in this category, the descriptions generally fit 24.7: standing water, 3; salt, 1; muddy, 1; backwater, 2; large, 4; small, 1.

25.1   <u>creek</u> /salt water; natural or man-made for ships?/

<u>cove</u> 38% P. VI

<u>inlet</u> 23% P. VI, XVIII

<u>bay</u> 16% P. XV, XVIII

<u>creek</u> 5% P. XIII

Descriptions:

<u>cove</u>: small (14); natural (25), man-made (3), either (2); protected (19).

<u>inlet</u>: natural (16); small (3); salt (2).

<u>bay</u>: large (15), "little bay" (5); natural (15), man-made (3), both (3); salt (2).

<u>creek</u>: in San Francisco used only in place names, e.g., Islais Creek.

25.2   <u>flat</u> /on mountain? on plains? fertile or barren?/

<u>plateau</u> 38% S.

<u>flat</u> (<u>lands</u>) 26% S.

<u>plain</u> 23% P. II, XVIIa

<u>mesa</u> 22% S. P. XIX

<u>prairie</u> 15% S. P. XVIII

<u>desert</u> 4% P. XIV

Description:

<u>plateau</u>: high altitude or mountain (43); barren (8), either (5); large (6).

25.2 cont.

> flat: high altitude (6), low (5); fertile (4), barren (7), either (2); small (5); in place names (4).
>
> plain: low altitude (7), either high or low (2); fertile (9), barren (15), either (10); large (5).
>
> mesa: high altitude (8); barren (7); large (3).
>
> prairie: low altitude (12); fertile (7), barren (8), either (2); large (3).

25.3   badlands /unfit for cultivation/
> wasteland 26% S. P. XIX
> alkali + (flats), (bed), (land), (ground), (soil) 22% S.
> desert (land) 22% P. VII

25.4   prairie /flat grassy country/
> prairie (land) 36% S.
> plains 33% P. IV
> meadow(s)/(land) 17% S. P. XVIIb

25.5   park /enclosed high altitude basin? any enclosed grassy place?/
> valley 71% G.C.-N.
> meadow 22% S. P. XVIIa
> Items 25.5-26.2 will be discussed as a group because of the close relationship of the terms in these categories.

25.6   canyon /deeply cut valley or gully; only between hills? narrow? steep sides? with stream?/
> canyon 80% G.C.-N.
> gorge 23% S.
> gully 12% S.
> gulch 8% (see 25.8)

25.7   ravine /deep narrow valley of a small stream/
> ravine 43% Note: 18 were given in response to 25.6 M.G.D.
> gorge 15% S.

25.8   gulch /in hillside? with stream? size? steep or sloping banks?/
> gulch 22% (see 25.6) S.
> No response 15%
> Many had used all their terms in the preceding items from 25.5.

26.1   <u>gully</u> /size?/

        <u>gully</u> 33% M.G.D.

        <u>wash</u> (<u>dry</u> ____) 21% S.

26.2   <u>arroyo</u> /depression with usually dry watercourse; size? steep or sloping banks?/

        <u>arroyo</u> 21% S.

Items 25.5-26.2 are treated together in a discussion of the meanings because of the overlapping use in these categories. By tabulating the terms used to describe the words most generally elicited, I was able to compile the following descriptions:

<u>canyon</u>	large; steep; narrow; deep; mountainous area; water present or optional.
<u>valley</u>	generally large but can be any size; flat; sloping sides; wide; water optional; mountainous area.
<u>gorge</u>	steep; narrow; deep; water present or optional; probably large.
<u>ravine</u>	small; narrow; steep or sloping; deep or shallow; water present or optional.
<u>gully</u>	small; shallow; probably sloping sides; dry or water optional; water-eroded; mountainous area.
<u>gulch</u>	small; narrow; dry or water optional; shallow; water-eroded; mountainous area; familiar now to many only in place names, such as <u>Polk Gulch</u>, used in San Francisco for Polk Street.
<u>wash</u>	small; flat; wide; probably dry but water optional; water-eroded; mountainous area; river-bed.
<u>arroyo</u>	usually dry but water optional; rocky; probably wide and flat; stream bed.
<u>meadow</u>	small; mountainous area.

Description of one item was often made in terms of one or more of the others. However, <u>valley</u> is apparently considered the generic term for the group because it is never used as a synonym in describing the others or in being described.

26.3   irrigation ditch
                irrigation ditch 60% G.C.-N.
                canal 34% S.
                ditch 32% S.
                sanky ("spelled zanja") 2% P. XV

26.5   notch /between mountains/
                pass 78% G.C.-N.
                notch 64% G.C.-N.
                Used only to mean a cut in a piece of wood.
                notch 15% S.
                gap 11% P. X, XIX
                cut 5% P. XIII, XVIII

26.6   We go for a swim to the) beach
                beach 75% G.C.-N.
                ocean 54% M.G.D.
                coast 6% P. XIII
                Note: The one San Francisco informant qualified his answer
                with "If I am inland."

26.7   wharf /where boats stop and freight is unloaded/
                wharf 55% G.C. P. XVIIa
                dock 54% G.C.-N.
                pier 45% M.G.D.

26.8   seawall /wall extending into the ocean/
                breakwater 54% M.G.D. P. XVIIa
                seawall 24% P. X

27.1   cement road
                cement 42% M.G.D.
                concrete 27% M.G.D.
                paved road 21% S.
                concrete road / highway / pavement 16% S.
                cement road 13% S.
                cement (to mean material only) 13% S.

27.2   black-top /bituminous/
                asphalt 41% M.G.D.
                black-top 30% M.G.D.

27.2 cont.

         macadam(ized) (road) 30% M.G.D. P. XVIII

         oil(ed) road 19% P. IV

         tar / tarred road 5% P. XIII

27.3   back road

         dirt road 51% G.C.-N.

         side road 23% S. P. XIX

         country road 20% S.

27.4   chuck hole /in road/

         chuck hole 63% G.C.-N.

         hole 21% S.

         rut 20% S.

27.5   The road was) slippery

         slippery 86% G.C.-N.

         slick 20% S.

27.6   parking strip /grass strip between sidewalk and street/

         No response 31% M.G.D.

         parkway 22% P. III, VI

         parking 14% S.

27.7   He threw a stone (at the dog

         threw 47% M.G.D.

         rock 88% G.C.-N.

27.8   He isn't) at home

         at home 56% G.C. P. XIX

         home 53% G.C.-N.

28.3   He was coming) towards (me

         toward 64% G.C.-N.

         towards 39% P. V

28.4   We named the child) for him

         after 90% G.C.-N.

         for 19% S. P. XVIIa

28.6   mongrel
            mongrel 80% G.C.-N.
            cur 27% S. P. XVIIa

28.8   He was) bitten (by a dog
            bitten 67% G.C.-N.
            bit 33% M.G.D.

29.2   bull /special words used by farmers? by women? in presence of
       women?/
            bull 98% G.C.-N.
            sire 4% P. XI, XIX
            Very few, perhaps a dozen, expressed any kind of taboo or
            special attitudes concerning this item.

29.3   calf /terms for female? male?/
            calf 97% G.C.-N.
            heifer (calf) 62% G.C.-N.
            Used generally to mean young female.
            bull-calf 35% G.C.-N.
            Used generally to mean young male.

29.4   Daisy is going) to calve
            have a calf 50% G.C.-N.
            to calve 23% S.
            to calf 15% S.

29.5   dogie /motherless calf/
            No response 33% S.
            orphan 19% S. P. XVIIb
            dogie 19% S. P. XIX
            maverick 15% S.
            leppy 9% P. VII, XI, XVIIb

29.7   stallion /special words used by farmers? by women? in presence
       of women?/
            stallion 72% G.C.-N.
            stud (horse) 30% M.G.D.
            Both terms were generally considered permissible in all
            company.

29.8   <u>bronco</u> /unbroken horse/

        <u>bronco</u> 58% M.G.D.

        <u>wild</u> (<u>horse</u>) 25% S. P. XVIIb

        <u>mustang</u> 14% P. II

29.9   <u>rodeo</u>

        <u>rodéo</u> 64% G.C. S. in Nevada

        <u>ródeo</u> 44% M.G.D.

30.1   <u>pinto</u> /mottled Indian pony; color combination?/

        <u>pinto</u> 81% G.C.-N.

        <u>paint</u> 11% S. P. XVIII

        The main color combinations given were: black and white,
108; brown and white, 74; any combination, 29; bay and
white, 21; red and white, 19; sorrel and white, 17.

        <u>Appaloosa</u> 3% P. XI, XVIIa

        Usually pronounced [æpə'lusɪˆ].

        "the spotted runner whose ancestors carried the Nez Perce
Indians under Chief Joseph into battle against the U. S.
Cavalry a century ago in Oregon. . . . The American variety
of the breed originated in the Palouse country of southeastern
Washington. Appaloosa, meaning 'spotted horse', is the deri-
vation of 'A Palouse' . . . . The runners come in assorted
colors—dun, sorrel, black, chestnut spots on a white blanket
. . . " From the San Francisco Chronicle, Aug. 8, 1966,
p. 54.

30.2   I have never) <u>ridden</u> (a horse

        <u>ridden</u> 82% G.C.-N.

        have) <u>rode</u> 20% S.

30.3   He fell) <u>off</u> (the horse /preposition, not adverb/

        <u>off</u> 86% G.C.-N.

        <u>off</u> <u>of</u> 16% S.

        (<u>got</u>) <u>bucked</u> <u>off</u> (<u>of</u>) 10% P. VIII, XVIIa

30.4   <u>to rear</u> /of a horse trying to throw the rider/

        <u>rear</u> (<u>up</u>) 90% G.C.-N.

        On hind legs.

30.4 cont.

      buck 86% G.C.-N.

      Front and back legs.

      sunfish 7% P. XI

      Meaning varied, but usually a twisting motion was described.

30.5   to shy /of a horse/

      to shy 89% G.C.-N.

30.6   hoofs

      hoofs 81% G.C.-N.

      hooves 22% S. P. XIX

30.7   horseshoes

      horseshoes 81% G.C.-N.

      shoes 30% P. III, XVIIb

30.8   horseshoes /game played with horseshoes/

      horseshoes 97% G.C.-N.

31.1   burro /small donkey/

      burro 74% G.C.-N.

      donkey 34% P. IV

      jackass 32% S.

31.2   ram /special words used by farmers? by women? in presence of women?/

      ram 80% G.C.-N.

      buck 29% S.

31.5   hog /male and female? old and young?/

      hogs 92% G.C.-N.

      Adult, male or female.

      pigs 40% S.

      Young, male or female.

      sows 34% P. V, VI

      Old female.

      shoats ([ʃʊɫts; ʃoᵘlts]) 7% P. XI, XVIIa

      Young female.

      gilts 3% P. VIII

31.6   boar /special words used by farmers? by women? in presence of
        women?/
                boar 76% G.C.-N.

31.8   tusks
                tusk(s) 85% G.C.-N.
                Seven San Francisco informants would use the term only in
                referring to elephants; there were 34 scattered responses
                of tusk for plural.

32.2   castrate /horses, bull-calves, boars, cats/
                castrate 68% G.C.-N.
                cut 26% M.G.D.
                alter 16% S. P. XVIIa
                spay 14% S.
                About one-third would use this term for females only; most
                used it for domestic animals, especially dogs and cats.

32.3   bawl /of calf being weaned/
                bawl 59% G.C.-N.
                No response 16%
                Of the 47 who had no term, 38 were urban.
                bellow 5% P. XI
                blat 5% P. XI

32.4   moo /during feeding time/
                moo 71% G.C.-N.
                No response 19%
                Thirty-five of the 58 were urban, especially in Los Angeles;
                there were also several in the lower San Joaquin Valley and
                across to Oxnard, as well as in Tonopah, Ely, and Pioche in
                Nevada.

32.5   bawl /of cow when calf is taken away/
                bawl 48% G.C. P. XVIIb
                No response 16%
                Again, of the 47 who gave no response, 38 were urban.

32.6   whinny /of horse during feeding time/
                whinny 41% P. V
                neigh 41% P. V, XIX

32.6 cont.

> nicker 18% S. P. XVIIa
>
> No response 15% S.

32.7   a setting-hen

> setting-hen 73% G.C.-N.

32.8   chicken coop

> chicken coop 70% G.C.-N.
>
> chicken house 34% M.G.D. P. XVIIa
>
> hen house 27% S.
>
> coop 17% P. IV

33.1   wish bone

> wish bone 98% G.C.-N.

33.2   chore time

> feeding time 45% M.G.D. P. XVIIb
>
> chore time 29% S.
>
> These two terms more or less complemented each other.
> Chore time was used particularly in the area between
> Mariposa and Selma, and was also more widely used in
> the southeastern part of the state.
>
> chores, (time to) do the chores 13% P. III

33.3   /calls to cows to get them from the pasture/

> No response 44% S.
>
> come boss(ie) 22% S. P. XVIIb
>
> here boss(ie) 15% P. II, XIX

33.4   /calls to cows to get them to stand still during milking/

> No response 39% S.
>
> so boss(ie) 31% M.G.D.

33.5   /calls to horses to get them from pasture/

> No response 59% M.G.D.
>
> call by name 28% P. II
>
> by whistling 19% S.

33.6 /calls to horses to urge them on/
　　　　get up 75% G.C.-N.
　　　　clucking 21% S.
　　　　giddy-up 14% S. [æ/ʌ/ə/ɛp]

33.7 /calls to horses to stop them/
　　　　whoa 94% G.C.-N.

33.8 /calls to pigs when feeding them/
　　　　No response 43% S.
　　　　pig pig 15% S.
　　　　suwee 14% S.

34.1 /calls to sheep to get them from the pasture/
　　　　No response 90% G.C.-N.
　　　　Ten percent said they would use dogs.

34.2 /calls to chickens when feeding them/
　　　　(come here) chick 74% G.C.-N.
　　　　Chick repeated usually two to five times.

34.3 reins /for driving or plowing, not riding/
　　　　reins 79% G.C.-N.
　　　　lines 35% M.G.D.

34.5 cinch /band that holds saddle on/
　　　　cinch 60% G.C.-N.
　　　　belly band 25% M.G.D. P. XVIIb

34.6 the near horse /horse on the left/
　　　　No response 35% Especially urban; rural scattered.
　　　　near horse 34% S. P. XVIIa
　　　　off horse 18% P. I
　　　　lead horse 17% S. P. XIX
　　　　wheel horse / wheeler 11% P. XI, XIX
　　　　nigh horse 6% P. VIII
　　　　Opinion was divided between left and right in all responses.

34.7 nose bag /bag attached to horse's head to feed him/
　　　　feed bag 58% M.G.D.
　　　　nose bag 41% M.G.D.

34.8   lariat /rope with loop; rawhide or hemp?/
                    lasso 69% G.C.-N.
                    The [u^u] sound was predominant in Northern California;
                    the [oʊ] sound appeared with greater frequency in Southern
                    California; there was about even distribution in Nevada.
                    lariat 54% P. V
                    reata 19% M.G.D. P. XVIIb
                    lass / lasso rope 15% S. (26 lass, 18 lasso)
                    lass was the predominant term in the northern rural area;
                    lasso was generally urban and southern.

35.1   It looks) good
                    good 75% G.C.-N.
                    well 15% S.

35.2   a little ways (over
                    a little ways 49% M.G.D.
                    a little way 21% S.
                    a short ways / way 22% P. V, XIX
                    a short distance 19% S. P. XVIIa

35.3   a long ways (to go
                    a long ways 53% G.C.-N.
                    a long way 34% M.G.D.

35.4   Two miles is) the farthest (he could go
                    as far as 49% M.G.D.
                    the farthest 19% P. VII, XIX
                    (Fartherest, 29; furtherest, 18; and furthest, 23 were found
                    mainly around Los Angeles in urban use; rural usage was
                    scattered from the north border to Pomona and Riverside
                    but did not occur in the southeast part except for one response
                    in Blythe. They were found in Austin, Tonopah, and Alamo
                    in Nevada.)

35.5   not a one
                    not a one 26% S.
                    negative verb (is/have) + any 25% S.
                    not any, 17, occurs in about the same general area.
                    none 24% S.

35.8   second cutting /of clover, grass/
              second crop 43% P. V
              second cutting 33% S.
              No response 25% S.

36.1   a sheaf (of wheat
              sheaf 28% S. P. XVIIa
              bundle 27% P. V
              No response 18% S.
              shock 13% P. XI

36.2   forty) bushels (of wheat
              bushels 73% G.C.-N.
              bushel 15% P. V, XIX
              (Note: Several mentioned that the term bushel was not
              commonly used in California; sacks, tons, etc. were more
              common. Sacks (12%) was especially common in Northern
              California valleys and along the central coast; also found
              in Banning and Elsinore.)

36.3   pick /to harvest grapes/
              pick 40% G.C.-N.
              cut 15% S.

36.4   pick /to harvest walnuts/
              pick 60% G.C.-N.
              gather 26% S.
              knock 16% S.

36.5   Oats) are thrashed
              are 68% G.C.-N.
              is / has been 18% S.

36.6   He isn't as tall) as I am
              as I am 66% G.C.-N.
              as I 22% S.
              as me 16% S.

36.7   It's) yours
              yours 98% G.C.-N.

36.8 When are) you-all (coming again? /is you-all ever used as singular?/

> you 79% G.C.-N.
>
> you-all 11%
>
> Most informants who gave this response qualified it by saying they used it only to a group, not in the southern sense, in a jocular sense, etc. Distribution was not significant.

37.1 you-all's /genitive/

> your(s) 73% G.C.-N.
>
> There were 42 instances of no response; in some instances this meant that the informant would not use any of the you-all forms.

37.2 who-all (was there?

> who 66% G.C.-N.
>
> who-all 30% S.
>
> Several who gave this response used the plural were with it; others said they would use it but "not in the Southern sense."

37.3 who-all's (children were there?

> whose 70% G.C.-N.
>
> what 16% S.

37.4 what-all (did he say?

> what 81% G.C.-N.
>
> what-all 11%
>
> Again informants qualified their responses with "for emphasis," "for clarity," "not in the Southern sense," etc.

37.5 white bread /white, in loaves/

> white bread 88% G.C.-N.
>
> bread 26% P. I
>
> light bread 7% P. XI, XVIIb

37.6 corn bread /in large cakes/

> corn bread 91% G.C.-N.

37.7   /other kinds of bread and cakes made of corn meal/
             No response 65% G.C.-N.

37.8   home-made bread and) bakery bread
             bakery bread 52% M.G.D.
             baker('s) bread 27% S.
             store bread 22% S. P. XVIIa
             boughten bread 12% P. XI

38.1   sweet roll
             snail 58% M.G.D. P. XVIIa
             coffee cake 40% M.G.D. P. XIX
             bear claw 28% S.
             cinnamon rolls 27% S. P. XVIIb
             sweet roll 16% S.
             butterhorn 15% P. X
             Danish pastry 4% P. XIII
             buns 4% P. XIII

38.2   doughnut /made with baking powder/
             doughnut 74% G.C.-N.
             cake doughnut 34% S.

38.3   doughnut /made with yeast/
             raised doughnut 60% G.C.-N.
             doughnut 34% S.

38.4   pancakes /of wheat/
             pancakes 75% G.C.-N.
             hot cakes 65% G.C.-N.
             Twenty-three use this term when ordering in a restaurant.
             flapjacks 23% P. IV
             Fourteen said this term would be used while camping,
             prospecting, etc.
             griddle cakes 10% P. XI, XVIII

38.5   recipe
             recipe 92% G.C.-N.
             receipt 11% P. IV, XVIIa
             Nine indicated this was old-fashioned and obsolete.

38.6   two pounds (of flour
            pounds 88% G.C.-N.
            (Only 6% used pound, foot, mile, ton, etc. These instances
            were widely scattered in California; in Nevada only one was
            reported—in Wells. Cf. 36.2.)

38.7   a cake) of yeast
            yeast 91% G.C.-N.
            east 13% S. P. XVIIa

38.8   liquid yeast /home-made; grows in jars?/
            No response 47% G.C. S. in Nevada
            sourdough 13% P. II, VI
            start(er) of yeast / starter yeast 12% P. XI
            potato yeast 10% P. XI

39.2   yolk
            yolk 91% G.C.-N.
            (There were scattered instances of yelk, 9%, and yulk, 6%.)

39.4   salt pork
            salt pork 68% G.C.-N.
            pork 20% S.
            (There was similarity of distribution for three terms:
            side-meat, 7 responses; side pork, 10 responses; sow belly,
            17 responses. All occurred in the Sacramento and San
            Joaquin Valleys, the Sierra, and the Desert areas. They
            were scattered in Nevada.)

39.5   bacon rind
            (bacon) rind 95% G.C.-N.
            skin 7% P. XI

39.6   a side (of bacon
            side 59% G.C.-N. P. XVIIa
            slab 57% G.C.-N.

39.7   chipped beef
            jerky 52% M.G.D. (Sixteen used this term for venison instead
            of beef.)

39.7 cont.

        chip beef 37% P. IV

        dried beef 33% P. II, VI

        chipped beef 26% S.

40.1   The meat is) spoiled

        spoiled G.C.-N.

        Three terms found scattered: rancid, 7%; spoilt, 10%; and
tainted, 6%. None of these was found in San Francisco. The
majority were found in rural Northern California and the
Pomona area, Nevada scattered.)

40.3   head cheese /pressed meat loaf made of hog's jowls, etc./

        head cheese 70% G.C.-N.

40.4   liverwurst

        liverwurst 81% G.C.-N.

        liver sausage 21% S.

40.5   scrapple /made of corn meal, meat juice, and scraps/

        No response 53% G.C.-N.

        scrapple 24% S. P. XVIIa

40.6   thick sour milk

        sour milk 54% M.G.D.

        clabber (milk) 30% S.

        clabbered (milk) 23% S. P. XVIIa

        curdled (milk) 18% P. X

40.7   The milk is) blinky /just turning sour/

        turned / turning (sour) 47% M.G.D.

        sour / soured / souring 30% S.

40.8   cottage cheese

        cottage cheese 94% G.C.-N.

        smear case 15% S. P. XVIIa

        Sixteen informants considered this an old-fashioned term.
There were four instances of initial [ʃ].

41.1   apple) <u>cobbler</u> /baked in a deep dish/

　　　　<u>cobbler</u> 76% G.C.-N.

　　　　<u>deep</u> (<u>dish</u>) (<u>apple</u>) <u>pie</u> 21% S.

41.2   <u>sauce</u> /sweet liquid served with pudding/

　　　　<u>sauce</u> 81% G.C.-N.

41.3   <u>frosting</u> /sweet coating of a cake/

　　　　<u>frosting</u> 76% G.C.-N.

　　　　<u>icing</u> 42% M.G.D.

41.6   a <u>snack</u> /food eaten between regular meals/

　　　　<u>snack</u> 72% G.C.-N.

　　　　<u>piece</u> / <u>piecing</u> / <u>piecemeal</u>(<u>ing</u>) 14% S.

　　　　<u>bite</u> (to eat) 13% P. X, XIX

41.7   I'm going) <u>to get</u> (supper

　　　　<u>to get</u> 50% G.C.-N.

　　　　<u>to fix</u> 22% S. P. XIX

　　　　<u>to cook</u> 17% S. P. XVIIa

　　　　<u>to prepare</u> 17% S. P. XIX

　　　　<u>to start</u> 10% P. X, XVIIa

　　　　(The use of <u>dinner</u>/<u>supper</u> was divided and scattered, <u>dinner</u>
　　　　69% and supper 39%. <u>Supper</u> was considered by many as old-
　　　　fashioned, a lighter meal, the evening meal. <u>Dinner</u> was more
　　　　widely used in urban areas.)

41.8   We) <u>ate</u> (at six o'clock

　　　　<u>ate</u> 94% G.C.-N.

42.1   How often) <u>have you eaten</u> (today?

　　　　<u>have you eaten</u> 85% G.C.-N.

　　　　<u>ate</u> / <u>eat</u> / <u>et</u> 16% S.

42.2   I'm going to) <u>make some coffee</u>

　　　　<u>make some coffee</u> 87% G.C.-N.

42.5   <u>I drank</u> (a lot of it

　　　　<u>I drank</u> 98% G.C.-N.

　　　　(There were only 6 responses of <u>I drunk</u>, all urban.)

42.6   How much) have you drunk?

    drank 56% G.C.-N.

    drunk 41% M.G.D.

    (Apparently some felt the word drunk taboo even in this context; one informant in Scotia said he would never use it because it meant tipsy; there were three instances of consumed and another of swallow because the informant wouldn't use drunk.)

42.7   soft drink

    soft drink 56% G.C.-N.

    soda pop 16% S. P. XVIII

    pop 16% S.

    soda 13% P. X, XVIII

42.8   I sat down

    I sat down 86% G.C.-N.

    set / sit 21% S.

43.1   warmed over /of food/

    warmed over 38% S.

    leftover(s) / food 31% P. IV, VI

    warmed up 26% S.

43.2   chew

    chew 99% G.C.-N.

43.3   vegetable garden

    vegetable garden 62% G.C.-N.

    garden 44% P. V

    home garden 4% P. XI

43.4   hominy grits /ground/

    No response 39% M.G.D.

    hominy 26% S.

    Sixteen said this would be whole, not ground.

    hominy grits 15% S.

    Four were familiar with this term because of eating it elsewhere.

43.6   Sugar is sold) <u>in</u> <u>bulk</u>
    <u>in</u> <u>bulk</u> 85% G.C.-N.

43.7   <u>jelly</u> /strained or unstrained/
    <u>jelly</u> 98% G.C.-N.
    <u>jam</u> 42% P. IV, VI
    Terms other than <u>jelly</u> may not have been deliberately
    elicited by the field worker. <u>Jam</u> was described as contain-
    ing fruit, unstrained.
    <u>preserves</u> 18% P. IV, VI
    Usually described as containing whole fruit.

44.1   <u>those</u> <u>boys</u>
    <u>those</u> <u>boys</u> 92% G.C.-N.
    <u>them</u> <u>boys</u> (or similar constructions from conversation)
    13% S.

44.2   It's) <u>over</u> <u>there</u>
    <u>over</u> <u>there</u> 91% G.C.-N.
    ((<u>way</u>) <u>over</u> <u>yonder</u>, 5%, and (<u>right</u>) <u>there</u>, 4%, were found
    only in California.)

44.3   <u>what's</u> <u>that</u>? /when failing to hear someone's utterance/
    <u>what</u>? 35% S.
    <u>hm</u>? 27% S.
    <u>huh</u>? 17% S.
    <u>pardon</u> (<u>me</u>)? 17% S.
    <u>what's</u> <u>that</u>? 16% S.

44.4   <u>whom</u> (do you want?
    <u>who</u> 83% G.C.-N.
    <u>whom</u> 19% S.

44.5   <u>pit</u> /of a cherry/
    <u>pit</u> 83% G.C.-N.
    <u>seed</u> 20% P. VI
    <u>stone</u> 17% S.

44.6   <u>pit</u> /of a peach/
    <u>pit</u> 60% G.C.-N.
    <u>stone</u> 40% M.G.D.
    <u>seed</u> 21% P. III, VI

44.7   cling-stone peach
                cling peach / clings 78% G.C.-N.
                cling-stone (peach) 43% M.G.D.

44.8   free-stone peach
                free-stone (peach) 96% G.C.-N.

45.1   apricot
                apricot [eɪ] 79% G.C.-N.
                apricot [æ] 24% S. P. XVIIa

45.2   peanuts
                peanuts 99% G.C.-N.

45.3   walnut shell /hard inner cover/
                (walnut) shell 99% G.C.-N.

45.4   walnut hull /green outer cover/
                (walnut) hull 39% M.G.D.
                husk 22% S.
                (Note: There were 39 who had no response for this item:
                of these, 20 were urban, 10 in Nevada.)

45.5   peanut shell
                (peanut) shell 96% G.C.-N.

45.7   praline /flat sheet of pecan candy/
                No response 41% G.C.-N.
                praline 29% S.
                For the most part, those who knew this word had learned
                of it from other places and were not very familiar with it.
                There was a great variety of pronunciations.

45.8   almonds
                almonds 99% G.C.-N.
                pine nuts / pie nuts 5% P. XIV, XVIII
                (An incidental item.)

46.3   green onions
                green onions 91% G.C.-N.

46.4   to) shell peas
            shell 87% G.C.-N.

46.5   butter beans /large, flat, yellow; not in pods/
            lima beans 67% G.C.-N.
            butter beans 31% M.G.D.

46.6   lima beans /smaller, green; not in pods/
            lima beans / limas 73% G.C.-N.
            baby lima(s) (beans) 13% S.

46.7   string beans
            string beans 94% G.C.-N.
            green beans 21% P. III

46.8   pinto beans
            pinto beans 33% S.
            pink beans 17% S. (None in Nevada.)
            No response 14% S.
            cranberry beans 8% P. XIII, XVIII
            frijoles 7%
            (speckled) bayos 6% P. VIII
            brown beans 6% P. VIII

47.1   husks /on ear of corn/
            husks 89% G.C.-N.

47.2   sweet corn /served on the cob/
            corn on the cob 75% G.C.-N.
            sweet corn 17% S.
            roasting ears 14% P. XI
            green corn 11% P. XI, XVIIa
            ears of corn 10% P. XI, XVIIa
            fresh corn 5% P. XI, XVIIa

47.3   tassel /top of corn stalk/
            tassel 85% G.C.-N.
            (corn) silk 11% P. X
            tassel (used only with other meanings, as on furniture or
            lamp) 11% S.

47.5   muskmelon
        cantaloupe 88% G.C.-N.
        muskmelon 44% M.G.D.
        Ten considered the word old-fashioned.
        mushmelon 24% S.
        Six considered this old-fashioned.

47.6   toadstool
        toadstool 96% G.C.-N.

47.8   a-singin' /verbs with the a- prefix/
        a-singin' 12% S.
        (The prefix form may not have been recorded by all field
        workers. It was combined with the -ing / -in' / contrast,
        which was more commonly recorded.)

48.2   /Negative of he ought to/
        ought not / oughtn't 61% G.C.-N.
        (Several gave simply ought not / oughtn't without completing
        the phrase. It was impossible to tell how many would use
        the to form and how many the simple form of the verb.)
        shouldn't 36% S.

48.4   I) might could (do it
        might be able to 40% M.G.D.
        might 39% M.G.D.
        may be able to 5%

48.5   woodpecker /get kinds/
        woodpecker 99% G.C.-N.
        yellow hammer 18% P. XI, XVIIa
        flicker 8% P. XI, XIX
        sapsucker 5% P. VIII

48.6   skunk
        skunk 98% G.C.-N.
        pole cat 27% S.
        civet (civic/civvy) cat 13% P. XI
        This was described as smaller than skunk or polecat, which
        were generally considered synonymous, although a few thought
        skunk the larger of the two.

48.7   chipmunk

   chipmunk 84% G.C.-N.

   gopher 12% P. VII

   Those who stated that this was a different animal from
   chipmunk (6 in all) were not included here.

   ground squirrel 11% P. III

   Eight stated this was not the same as chipmunk.

48.8   varmints

   pests 68% G.C.-N.

   varmints 17% S.

   rodent 16% S. P. XVIIa

49.1   shrimp

   shrimp 71% G.C.-N.

   prawn(s) 33% S.

   shrimps 29% M.G.D.

   prongs 5% P. X

   The general distinction made between shrimp and prawn
   was in size, prawn being considered much larger. A few
   mentioned that prawn would be found in Louisiana or on
   the gulf.

49.4   crawfish

   crawfish 40% M.G.D. in Northern California; S. otherwise

   No response 19% S.

   lobster 13% P. XIII

   Thirteen percent of the informants were also familiar with
   the terms crawdad and crayfish, both scattered throughout
   the state. Five informants said that crawfish was the same
   as the western lobster, 14 that it was smaller (or small),
   16 that it was fresh water, 15 that it was edible, and 7 that
   it was used for fish bait. Eleven San Francisco informants
   used lobster for the eastern or western variety. This meaning was also found in the North Bay area.

49.5   toad

   toad 87% G.C.-N.

   (Twenty-six (9%) responded with frog; 20 of these responses
   were urban, 14 from Los Angeles.)

49.6   horned toad /small flat lizard with horns on head and back/
             horn toad 48% M.G.D.
             horned toad 24% P. VI
             horny toad 20% P. VII

49.7   earthworm
             angleworm 63% G.C.-N.
             worm 57% G.C.-N.
             earthworm 29% S.
             fishworm / fishing worm 19% P. XI, XVIII
             garden worm 2% P. XII

49.8   night crawler /large earthworm/
             No response 78% G.C.-N.
             night crawler 12% S.
             Several mentioned knowing about them because of having
             seen them in other places, especially Oregon, but the item
             was not found on the North Border.

50.1   minnows /for bait/
             minnows 76% G.C.-N.
             shiners 7% P. XIII, XVIIa

50.2   terrapin
             turtle 63% G.C.-N.
             tortoise 16% S.
             land turtle 15% S.

50.3   rattlesnake /get varieties/
             rattlesnake 93% G.C.-N.
             rattler 27% S.
             diamond back (rattler) 21% S.
             There were 8 responses each of diamond (rattler) and
             diamond head, 9 of black diamond (rattler).
             sidewinder 19% S.
             timber rattler 5% P. XIV

50.4   moths /in clothes/
             moths 98% G.C.-N.
             millers 8% P. X.

50.5   lightning bug

        firefly 52% M.G.D.

        glowworm 22% P. X, XIX

        At the time this material was collected, the song "Glowworm" was very popular and apparently accounted for many of these responses. Several qualified their response as not the same thing as lightning bug.

        ligntning bug 20% S.

        Few had really seen one. Those who were familiar with them had usually seen them elsewhere.

50.6   dragon fly

        dragon fly 59% G.C. S. in Nevada

        (devil's) darning needle 15% S.

        Four were told as children that the darning needle would darn their ears, mouths, or eyes up. See ear sewer below.

        mosquito hawk 7% P. XI

        ear sewer 6% P. XIII

        snake doctor 5% P. VIII

        The San Francisco, Los Angeles, and Nevada informants (3) were Negroes.

        snake feeder 3% P. XI

50.7   wasps

        wasps 90% G.C.-N.

        mud dauber 11% P. XI, XIX

        yellow jacket 6% S.

50.8   hornets

        hornets 70% G.C.-N.

        (There were 12 replies of yellow jacket for this item.)

51.1   yellow jackets

        yellow jackets 68% G.C.-N.

        (Many informants referred back to 50.7 and 50.8.)

Descriptions for 50.7, 50.8, and 51.1

1. Synonyms:	wasp	hornet	yellow jacket	mud dauber
wasp	--	20	40	11
hornet	5	-	13	-
yellow jacket	13	7	-	5
mud dauber	3	-	2	-
bee	-	4	-	-

2. Color:				
yellow	51	17	62	2
yellow and black	33	11	36	5
yellow and brown	8	1	4	1
black	24	34	-	5
other varied	20	7	-	-
other (gray, brown, etc.)	16	20	5	1

3. Location of nest:				
around buildings	52	16	21	1
ground, old trees, logs	12	12	30	-
trees	38	31	13	-
near water	1	-	4	-

4. Material of nest:				
mud	79	28	28	21
paperlike	38	28	27	-

5. Shape:				
wasp-waist	15	1	-	1
large	23	46	13	-
small	22	8	21	4
long	50	16	9	1
short	5	5	-	-
slender	47	7	16	2
fat	5	17	9	-

6. Stings:				
yes	58	38	29	4
no	-	-	2	4

7. Meat eater:	-	-	3	-

8. No honey:	-	6	3	-

51.2   chigger /small insect burrowing in human flesh/
            No response 39% S.
            (wood) tick 22% P. X
            (wood tick only 5% P. XIII)
            chigger / jigger 19% S.

51.3   spiderweb /indoors/
            cobweb 70% G.C.-N.
            spiderweb 50% M.G.D.
            web 15% P. VII

51.4   spiderweb /outdoors/
            spider('s) web 69% G.C. S. in Nevada
            cobweb 32% S.
            web 9% P. VII

51.6   sugar maple
            maple(tree) 71% G.C.-N.
            sugar maple 20% S.
            No response 14% S.

51.7   maple grove
            (maple) grove 44% M.G.D.
            No response 36% S.
            (maple) orchard 19% P. IV, VI

51.8   sycamore
            sycamore 47% S.
            plane / Oriental plane 5% P. XIII

52.4   Some berries are) poisonous
            poisonous 62% G.C. S. in Nevada
            poison 40% M.G.D.

52.5   I must ask my) husband
            husband 94% G.C.-N.

52.6   I must ask my) wife
            wife 93% G.C.-N.

52.7 <u>widow</u>

> <u>widow</u> 99% G.C.-N.

52.8 /what do you call your <u>father</u>?/

> <u>dad</u> 59% G.C.-N.
> <u>papa</u> 40% S.
> This term was generally used as a child and now considered old-fashioned.
> <u>father</u> 37% S.
> <u>daddy</u> 17% S. P. XVIII
> Thirteen used this term as a child.
> <u>pa</u> 11% P. VII, XVIII

53.1 /what do you call your <u>mother</u>?/

> <u>mother</u> 64% G.C.-N.
> <u>mama</u> M.G.D.
> Generally used as a child.
> <u>mom</u> 26% S.
> <u>ma</u> 16% P. VII, XIX

53.2 <u>parents</u> /immediate family/

> <u>parents</u> 56% G.C.-N.
> <u>folks</u> 39% S.
> <u>family</u> 25% P. X, XIX

53.3 her <u>relatives</u> /others related by blood/

> <u>relatives</u> 75% G.C.-N.
> <u>relations</u> 26% S.
> <u>family</u> 12% P. X, XVIIa
> <u>folks</u> 10% P. XI

53.4 <u>grandfather</u>

> <u>grandpa</u> 55% M.G.D.
> <u>grandfather</u> 45% M.G.D.

53.5 <u>grandmother</u>

> <u>grandma</u> 62% G.C.-N.
> <u>grandmother</u> 44% M.G.D.

53.7   baby carriage

baby buggy 73% G.C.-N.

(buggy 12% S.)

baby carriage 32% S.

53.8   midwife

midwife 90% G.C.-N.

54.1   The boy) resembles (his father

looks like 64% G.C.-N.

resembles 61% G.C.-N.

takes after 21% S.

acts like 8% P. XV

is (just) like 6% P. XV

To refer to appearance, 50 would use resembles, 51 would use looks like; to refer to disposition, 11 would use acts like, 12 is just like, and 23 takes after. The last term would be used by 10 to mean both appearance and disposition.

54.2   She has) raised (three children

raised 88% G.C.-N.

brought up 19% S. P. XVIIa

reared 15% S. P. XVIIa

54.3   You've) grown (big

grown (up) 97% G.C.-N.

54.4   bastard /illegitimate child/

bastard 58% G.C.-N.

illegitimate (child) 42% P. VII, XIX

catch-colt 3% P. XIV

Approximately one-third of those responding with bastard qualified it as a curse word and 20 said they wouldn't use it.

54.8   partner

partner 67% G.C.-N.

pardner 45% M.G.D.

Of those using partner, 35 would use it in the vocative, 75 would not. Of those who gave pardner, 33 would use it in the vocative, 56 would not. Many of those who said that they would use the word in the vocative qualified it as a jocular term.

55.5   jackleg preacher /untrained, part-time/

        No response 78% G.C.-N.

55.6   student

        student 82% G.C.-N.

        pupil 49% M.G.D.

        scholar 29% S. P. XVIIa

        school boy / girl 8% P. II, XVIIa

55.7   The boy has a) paper route

        [$ra^{+}t$] 82% G.C.-N.

        [$ru^{u}t$] 21% S. P. XVIIa

        [$ra^{+}t$] of a trip 24% S.

        [$ru^{u}t$] of a trip 24% S. P. XIX

        It is possible that not all field workers asked for the second
meaning, in which case the similarity of distribution could
be accounted for.

56.1   postman

        mailman 73% G.C.-N.

        postman 33% S.

        mail carrier 29% M.G.D. P. XVIIa

        letter carrier 7% P. XIII

56.2   cowboy

        cowboy 81% G.C.-N.

        buckaroo 16% P. XI, XVIIb

        cowhand 9% P. II, VI

        cow puncher 9% P. II

        vaquero 7% S. (see borrowings) P. XVIII

        (Compare with buckaroo above.)

        Sixty informants said that a cowboy would ride only; 32 that
he would do all kinds of work. Ranch hand (6% scattered),
was mentioned as the one who did the other work on the ranch.

        herdsman 2% P. XI

56.3   hand /on a farm or ranch/

        ranch hand 43% M.G.D.

        farm hand 33% S.

        hired man 31% S. P. XIX

        roustabout 4% P. XIV

        chore man 3% P. XIV

56.4 <u>Negro</u> /neutral terms/

> <u>Negro</u> 91% G.C.-N.
>
> <u>colored</u> <u>man</u> / <u>person</u> / <u>people</u> / <u>folks</u> 34% S. P. XIX

56.5 <u>Negro</u> /derogatory/

> <u>nigger</u> 72% G.C.-N.
>
> Although many gave this response, quite a few also said they would not use it.
>
> <u>No</u> <u>response</u> 11% S.
>
> <u>coon</u> 8% P. X, XVIIa

56.6 <u>a</u> <u>rustic</u> /derogatory and neutral terms/

> <u>hick</u> 30% S.
>
> <u>hillbilly</u> 18% S. P. XIX
>
> <u>farmer</u> 15% S. P. XIX
>
> This term was generally considered neutral, but 5 San Franciscans and 1 informant from Yerington considered it derogatory; one from Los Angeles "slightly derogatory."
>
> <u>hayseed</u> 15% S.
>
> <u>country</u> <u>hick</u> 11% S. (see <u>hick</u> above)
>
> <u>Okies</u> 12% P. XII, XVIIa
>
> <u>rancher</u> 5% P. XI
>
> <u>Arkie</u> 2% P. XII

56.7 <u>out</u> <u>in</u> <u>the</u> <u>sticks</u>

> <u>out</u> <u>in</u> <u>the</u> <u>sticks</u> / <u>in</u> <u>the</u> <u>sticks</u> 70% G.C.-N.
>
> <u>out</u> <u>in</u> <u>the</u> <u>country</u> / <u>in</u> <u>the</u> <u>country</u> 24% S.

56.8 <u>migratory</u> <u>worker</u> /neutral and derogatory terms/

> <u>transient</u> (<u>worker</u>) / (<u>laborer</u>) 20% S.
>
> <u>migratory</u> <u>worker</u> 19% S. in California; none in Nevada
>
> <u>fruit</u> <u>tramp</u> 16% P. XI
>
> <u>migrant</u>(<u>s</u>) (<u>worker</u>) 13% P. II
>
> (Note: Ten percent gave <u>Okies</u> in this category; again over half were urban, 12 of which were from San Francisco. Of 5 <u>Arkie</u> responses, 1 was urban, 2 rural, and 2 Nevada.)

57.1 <u>Mexican</u> /neutral and derogatory terms/

> <u>Mexican</u> 94% G.C.-N.
>
> <u>wetback</u> 44% M.G.D.
>
> <u>greaser</u> 23% S. P. XVIIa

57.1 cont.

> cholo 11% P. VII
>
> Generally considered derogatory.
>
> (Mexican) national 8% P. XI

57.2   I) almost fell down

> almost fell 47% G.C.-N.
>
> almost fell down 22% G.C.-N.
>
> nearly fell (down) 16% P. III, XVIIb

57.5   look here /exclamation/

> look here 48% M.G.D.
>
> look at this / that 18% P. II, VI

57.7   either you or I (will have to do it

> either you or I 63% G.C.-N.
>
> either you or me 15% S.

57.8   neither you nor I (can do anything about it

> neither you nor I 35% S.
>
> neither you or I 28% S.

58.3   beard

> whiskers 3% P. XI

58.5   gums

> [guᵘmz] 3% P. XVI

59.1   haunches

> haunches 85% G.C.-N.

59.2   strong

> strong 97% G.C.-N.
>
> husky 16% S.
>
> powerful 8% P. VIII, XVIIa
>
> muscular 5% P. VIII

59.3   stingy

> stingy 68% G.C.-N.
>
> tight 55% G.C.-N.
>
> tightwad 19% S. P. XIX
>
> miserly 17%; a miser 10% S.

59.5 She's quite) <u>lively</u> /of young people/
        <u>active</u> 47% M.G.D.
        <u>lively</u> 24% S. P. XIX
        <u>peppy</u> /<u>full</u> <u>of</u> <u>pep</u> 23% S.

59.6 She's quite) <u>lively</u> /of old people/
        <u>active</u> 54% M.G.D.
        <u>spry</u> 42% S.
        <u>lively</u> 13% S. P. XIX

59.7 I'm) <u>afraid</u>
        <u>scared</u> 63% G.C.-N.
        <u>afraid</u> 38% M.G.D.
        <u>frightened</u> 14% S.

59.8 She) <u>didn't</u> <u>use</u> <u>to</u> (be afraid /negative of <u>used</u> <u>to</u>/
        <u>didn't</u> <u>use</u> <u>to</u> 43% M.G.D.
        <u>never</u> <u>used</u> <u>to</u> <u>do</u> <u>it</u> 16% S.
        <u>never</u> <u>was</u> / <u>was</u> <u>never</u> 10% S.
        <u>wasn't</u> 10% S.

60.2 Don't be so) <u>obstinate</u>
        <u>stubborn</u> 83% G.C.-N.
        <u>obstinate</u> 18% S. P. XVIIa
        <u>set</u> (<u>in</u> <u>his</u> <u>ways</u>) 14% P. II
        <u>ornery</u> / <u>onery</u> 11% P. XI

60.3 He got awfully) <u>angry</u>
        <u>mad</u> 76% G.C.-N.
        <u>angry</u> 58% G.C.-N.
        <u>hot</u> (<u>around</u> / <u>under</u> <u>the</u> <u>collar</u>) 4% P. XIV
        <u>peeved</u> 3% P. VIII
        <u>excited</u> 2% P. VIII

60.4 <u>keep</u> <u>calm</u>
        <u>keep</u> <u>calm</u> 70% G.C.-N.
        <u>calm</u> <u>down</u> 19% S.

60.5 <u>tired</u> /normal and strong terms/
        <u>tired</u> (<u>out</u>) 92% G.C.-N.
        <u>pooped</u> (<u>out</u>) 35% S.

60.5 cont.

      exhausted 30% S. P. XIX

      all in 25% S.

      worn out 20% S.

      corked 3% P. XIII

60.6   lazy

      lazy 98% G.C.-N.

      indolent 5% P. IX

60.7   goose pimples

      goose pimples 76% G.C.-N.

      goose flesh 24% S.

60.8   She) got sick

      got sick 57% M.G.D.

      took sick / ill 19% P. III, XIX

      became ill 16% P. II, VI, XIX

      was taken sick / ill 15% S. P. XVIIa

      became sick 7% P. I, XIX

61.1   He) caught a cold

      caught cold 55% G.C.-N.

      caught a cold 38% S. P. XIX

      took (a) cold 13% P. X

61.4   Haven't you) taken (your medicine yet?

      taken 96% G.C.-N.

61.5   I) took (it this morning

      took 97% G.C.-N.

61.6   deaf

      deaf 97% G.C.-N.

      (Pronunciation of [dif] was given by 40 informants scattered.)

      hard of hearing 56% M.G.D.

      When a distinction was made, this term was usually con-
sidered to indicate partial impairment of hearing, deaf total.

61.7   He) <u>sweated</u> (hard
                  <u>sweat</u> 70% G.C.-N.
                  <u>perspired</u> 19% P. VII
                  <u>sweated</u> 17% S.
                  Fifteen informants said <u>sweat</u> would be used only in reference
                  to animals.

62.1   I don't know what he) <u>died</u> <u>of</u>
                  <u>died</u> <u>of</u> 70% G.C.-N.
                  <u>died</u> <u>from</u> 29% P. I, XIX

62.2   <u>cemetery</u>
                  <u>cemetery</u> 97% G.C.-N.
                  <u>graveyard</u> 32% M.G.D.
                  Seventeen mentioned that this word was old-fashioned.
                  <u>burial</u> <u>ground</u>(<u>s</u>) 4% P. VIII, XVIIa
                  <u>potters</u> <u>field</u> 4% P. XII
                  Used for burial of paupers only.

62.3   <u>casket</u>
                  <u>coffin</u> 67% G.C.-N.
                  Thirteen, 8 of them in San Francisco, regarded this word
                  as old-fashioned.
                  <u>casket</u> 62% G.C.-N.

62.7   <u>jaundice</u>
                  <u>jaundice</u> 49% M.G.D.
                  <u>yellow</u> <u>jaundice</u> 48% M.G.D.
                  <u>yellow</u> <u>janders</u> / <u>jaunders</u> 5% P. XIII

62.8   <u>vomit</u> /neutral and polite terms/
                  <u>vomit</u> 90% G.C.-N.
                  <u>throw</u> <u>up</u> 43% S.
                  <u>heave</u> 8% P. II

63.1   <u>throw</u> <u>up</u> /crude and jocular terms/
                  <u>puke</u> 38% M.G.D.
                  <u>throw</u> <u>up</u> 34% M.G.D.
                  Thirty-one referred to response for 62.8 and had no other
                  terms. Twenty-two would give no response to this category.
                  <u>heave</u> 27% S. P. XIX
                  <u>vomit</u> 3% P. XIII

63.2   He is sick) <u>to his stomach</u>
                    <u>to his stomach</u> 51% G.C.-N.
                    <u>at his stomach</u> 41% M.G.D.

63.3   <u>I shall be</u> (disappointed if he doesn't come
                    <u>I'll be</u> 63% G.C.-N.
                    <u>will</u> 35% M.G.D.
                    <u>shall</u> 14% S.

63.4   <u>we shall be</u>
                    <u>we'll be</u> 58% G.C.-N.
                    <u>will</u> 38% M.G.D.
                    (Seven percent responded with <u>shall</u>.)

63.5   He is) <u>courting her</u>
                    <u>courting</u> 57% M.G.D.
                    <u>going with</u> 29% S. P. XIX
                    <u>going steady (with)</u> 15% S.
                    <u>sparking</u> 8% P. XI
                    The two Oceanside informants qualified the term as jocular,
                    old-fashioned, and obsolete.
                    <u>calling on</u> 6% P. XIV
                    <u>going together</u> 4% P. XV

63.6   She) <u>turned him down</u>
                    <u>turned him down</u> 29% S.
                    <u>jilted</u> 24% S.
                    <u>broke off (with him)</u> 17% S. P. XIX
                    <u>threw him over</u> 16% S.
                    There were 68 responses with variations of <u>gave him</u> (the
                    <u>gate</u>, <u>the air</u>, <u>the brush-off</u>, <u>the cold shoulder</u>, <u>ditch</u>, <u>sack</u>,
                    <u>heave</u>, <u>mitten</u>—the most popular being <u>the air</u>, 25, and <u>the
                    gate</u>, 24.)

63.7   <u>married</u>
                    <u>married</u> 99% G.C.-N.
                    <u>hitched (up)</u> 20% S. P. XVIIa
                    <u>tied (up)</u> / <u>tied the knot</u> 8% P. XIV
                    <u>wed(ded)</u> 4% P. IX, XVIIa

63.8   shivaree /noisy, burlesque serenade after wedding/
            shivaree 76% G.C.-N.
            There were 24 with no response, all but 1 urban.
            About 10 said the word was old-fashioned or out-dated.
            reception 4% P. XIV
            One said this was not the same as shivaree, another that
            it was a new term.

64.1   a dance
            dance 98% G.C.-N.
            ball 20% S. P. XVIIb
            shindig 13% P. XI, XVIIa
            hoedown 4% P. XIV

64.2   He) skipped class
            played hookey 86% G.C.-N.
            cut class / school 18% P. X
            ditched 14% P. VII
            played / was truant 9% P. X, XVIIa
            sloughed school 1% P. XVI, XIX [slʌft]

64.3   education
            education 96% G.C.-N.

64.4   grammar school
            grammar school 75% G.C.-N.
            elementary school 28% S. P. XIX
            grade school 26% S.
            primary (school) / (grades) 17% S. P. XVIIa
            public school 4% P. IX

64.5   first grade
            first grade 92% G.C.-N.
            primary (grade) / (class) / (department) 11% P. XIII

65.3   theater
            theater 33% M.G.D.
            opera house 13% P. II, VI, XVIIa
            show house 7% P. VIII
            play house 6% P. VIII, XVIIa
            Thirteen considered opera house an old-fashioned term;
            three, play house.

65.4   railway station
            depot 79% G.C.-N.
            station 37% S.
            railroad station 22% S.

65.5   <u>town</u> <u>square</u>
       <u>park</u> 47% M.G.D.
       <u>public</u> <u>square</u> / <u>city</u> <u>square</u> 31% S.
       <u>plaza</u> 29% S. (see Borrowings)
       <u>civic</u> <u>center</u> 18% S.

65.6   <u>kitty</u>-<u>cornered</u> /of walking across intersection or lot/
       <u>catty</u>-<u>corner</u>(ed) 40% M.G.D.
       (Twelve percent gave <u>cate</u>(<u>r</u>)-<u>cornered</u> with similar or
       sometimes complementary distribution.)
       <u>kitty</u>-<u>corner</u>(ed) 27% S.
       <u>diagonal</u>(<u>ly</u>) 17% S.

65.7   on the) <u>street</u> <u>car</u>
       <u>street</u> <u>car</u> 94% G.C.-N.
       <u>trolley</u>(<u>car</u>) 24% S.
       (Only 7 mentioned <u>cable</u> <u>car</u>: 6 in Northern California
       between Alturas and Placerville, 1 in Los Angeles, none
       in San Francisco.)

65.8   I) <u>want</u> <u>to</u> <u>get</u> <u>off</u> (at the next corner
       <u>want</u> <u>to</u> <u>get</u> <u>off</u> 81% G.C.-N.
       <u>want</u> <u>off</u> 15% S.

66.1   <u>law</u> <u>and</u> <u>order</u> (a pronunciation item)
       (Ten responses of <u>peace</u> <u>and</u> <u>order</u> were given: Los Angeles,
       East Bay, and Sacramento, Markleeville - Modesto south to
       Elsinore; Carson City and Pioche.)

67.1   <u>Washington</u> (for state), <u>Washington</u>, <u>D</u>. <u>C</u>.
       <u>Washington</u> 92% G.C.-N.

67.5   <u>Los</u> <u>Angeles</u>
       <u>Los</u> <u>Angeles</u> 85% used [ndʒ]; 14% used [ŋ / ŋg] G.C.-N.
       <u>L</u>.<u>A</u>. 65% G.C.-N.
       Opinion was divided on the desirability of abbreviations.
       <u>San</u> <u>Bernardino</u> 93% G.C.-N.
       <u>San</u> <u>Berdoo</u> 28% S.
       (In San Bernardino itself there were 2 responses, 1 of
       <u>Berdoo</u> alone, the other <u>San</u> <u>Berdoo</u>, qualified with the
       remark that "natives don't say this.")

67.7   San Francisco

San Francisco 99% G.C.-N.

Frisco 44% M.G.D.

the city 19% P. XIV, XVIII

S.F. 16% P. II, VI, XVIIa

San Fran 2% P. XIV

Fourteen in San Francisco expressed dislike of nicknames, especially Frisco.

68.1   I like him) because (he's . . .

because 90% G.C.-N.

'cause / cuz 21% S.

68.6   my God! /an oath/

my God! 35% S.

God! 26% S.

good God! 4% P. XIII

68.7   devil /also veiled and jocular terms/

devil 99% G.C.-N.

Satan 33% S.

boogey man 29% S.

bugaboo 8% P. X

68.8   ghosts

ghosts 90% G.C.-N.

spooks 24% S.

69.2   It's) rather (cold

rather 37% S.

kind of 33% S.

pretty 18% P. II

a little 17% S.

fairly 7% P. XIII

69.4   certainly! /strong affirmation/

sure 37% M.G.D.

certainly 25% S.

69.5   yeah /habitual forms of "yes"/

yeah 56% M.G.D.

(includes vowel variations of: [æ, ɛ, ə, æə, ɛə])

69.5 cont.

        m-hm 52% G.C.-N.

        yes 43% M.G.D.

        uh-huh 30% S.

        [jæl / ɪ jæl] 16% P. II

69.6   /do you habitually say "yes, sir" and "yes, ma'am" or simply "yes"?/

        Forty-two percent said that they did not use the terms, 22% that they did, at least occasionally. Ten percent would use them as a term of respect to older people, women, etc. Nine percent used them in business, 4% for emphasis, and 3% had used them as children. There were no geographic patterns.

69.7   no /habitual forms of negation/

        no 74% G.C.-N.

        [ʔmʔm / hmʔm] 32% P. II

        huh-uh / uh-uh 26% S. P. XIX

        nope 12% P. X

69.8   how are you? /to an intimate friend/

        how are you? 59% G.C.-N.

        how are you feeling / how you feeling? 12% 9% S.

70.1   how do you do? /to a stranger/

        how do you do? 61% G.C.-N.

        (I'm) pleased to meet you 17% S.

70.2   come again! /to a visitor/

        come again 52% M.G.D.

        come back (again) (soon) 35% S.

70.3   Merry Christmas!

        Merry Christmas! 97% G.C.-N.

        (Five informants said they had heard of Christmas gift; they used Merry Christmas!, however.)

70.8   dime store /store where all kinds of cheap goods are sold/

        dime store 38% M.G.D.

        five and ten 37% M.G.D. P. XIX

70.8 cont.

five and ten cent store 10% M.G.D.

variety (store) 22% S. P. XVIIa

five and dime (store) 20% S.

Woolworth's 16% S. P. XVIIa

(Kress's was given by 8 informants, 4 from Los Angeles,
1 Sacramento, 1 San Diego, and 2 El Cerrito.)

fifteen cent store 5% P. VIII

notion store 4% P. XIV, XVIII

novelty store 3% P. XIV, XVIIa

71.1   coast lying down

No response 42% M.G.D.

belly flop 36% S.

There is some question as to the reliability of this item,
inasmuch as several informants qualified it as meaning a
bad dive into water.

belly-bust(er) 6% P. IX, XVIIa

Again, the one informant from San Diego qualified this as
meaning to hit flat after a dive.

71.2   somersault

somersault 91% G.C.-N.

tumblesault 3% P. XIII

(Two responses in the East Bay, one tumblesauce, the other
simple tumble; Banning also gave tumble only.)

71.3   I swam across

swam 93% G.C.-N.

swum 7% S.

71.4   he dived in

dove 79% G.C.-N.

dived 23% S.

71.5   he was drowned

drowned 82% G.C.-N.

drownded 13% S.

71.6   marbles

          marbles 99% G.C.-N.

          agates 59% P. VI

          taw(s) 27% P. I

          glassies 23% P. VI

          dobies 18% S.

          dobabies / dobabes 4% P. XI

          Made of cheap clay.

          migs 11% P. XV

          aggies 10% P. XII

          steelies 7% P. XI

          chinas / chinies 6% P. XIII

          shooters 5% P. XI

          puries 4% P. X

          crystal 3% P. XIV

          potteries 3% P. XVI

71.7   starting line /in marbles/

          No response 32% S.

          taw (line) 21% S.

          (There were 5 scattered responses, 1 urban, of toe line /

          mark.)

          lag(ging) line 19% S. P. XIX

71.8   The baby) creeps (on the floor

          crawls 82% G.C.-N.

          creeps 46% M.G.D.

72.1   He) climbed (up a tree

          climbed 88% G.C.-N.

          clum 12% S.

          Four said it with amusement.

72.2   I have often climbed up

          have climbed 87% G.C.-N.

          clum 11% S.

72.3   She) kneeled (down

          knelt 67% G.C.-N.

          kneeled 39% M.G.D.

72.4   I'm going to) <u>lie</u> <u>down</u>
                 <u>lie</u> <u>down</u> 76% G.C.-N.
                 <u>lay</u> <u>down</u> 29% S.

72.5   He) <u>lay</u> (in bed all day
                 <u>laid</u> 59% G.C.-N.
                 <u>lay</u> 35% S.
                 <u>stayed</u> 14% S.

72.6   I) <u>dreamed</u> (all night
                 <u>dreamed</u> 81% G.C.-N.
                 <u>dreamt</u> 50% (includes [mpt] pronunciation) M.G.D.
                 <u>dremp</u> 10%

72.7   <u>I</u> <u>woke</u> <u>up</u> <u>early</u>
                 <u>woke</u> <u>up</u> 73% G.C.-N.
                 <u>awakened</u> 14% S.
                 <u>awoke</u> 13% P. X

72.8   <u>stamp</u> (the floor
                 <u>stomp</u> 53% G.C.-N.
                 <u>stamp</u> 51% M.G.D.

73.1   May I) <u>take</u> <u>you</u> <u>home</u>? /on foot or in a vehicle?/
                 <u>take</u> <u>you</u> <u>home</u> 53% M.G.D.
                 By car, 42; on foot, 1; both, 26.
                 <u>help</u> <u>you</u> <u>home</u> 24% P. II, VI
                 On foot, 43; by car, 2; both, 3.
                 <u>see</u> <u>you</u> <u>home</u> 16% P. VII, XVIII
                 On foot, 16; by car, 1; both, 5.
                 <u>give</u> <u>you</u> <u>a</u> <u>lift</u> 15% P. II, VI, XVIIa
                 By car, 25.
                 <u>give</u> <u>you</u> <u>a</u> <u>ride</u> (<u>home</u>) 14% P. IV, VI
                 By car, 24.
                 <u>drive</u> 6% P. VII
                 By car, 11.

73.4   I) <u>lugged</u> (the suitcase down to the station
                 <u>carried</u> 83% G.C.-N.
                 <u>lugged</u> 28% S. P. XVIIa
                 <u>packed</u> 20% P. IV

73.5   <u>go</u> <u>bring</u> (me a knife

  <u>bring</u> 33% M.G.D.

  <u>go</u> <u>get</u> 32% S. P. XVIII

  (There were 31 scattered responses of <u>go</u> <u>and</u> <u>get</u>.)

  <u>get</u> 30% S.

73.7   Who) <u>caught</u> (it?

  <u>caught</u> 98% G.C.-N.

73.8   I'll wait) <u>for</u> <u>you</u>

  <u>for</u> <u>you</u> 98% G.C.-N.

74.1   in good) <u>humor</u>

  <u>in</u> <u>good</u> <u>humor</u> 83% G.C.-N.

  <u>good</u> <u>mood</u> 22% S.

  <u>in</u> <u>good</u> / <u>high</u> <u>spirits</u> 21% S. P. XVIIa

  <u>frame</u> <u>of</u> <u>mind</u> 5% P. XIV

74.2   Who) <u>taught</u> (you that?

  <u>taught</u> 95% G.C.-N.

74.3   We) <u>intend</u> (to go soon

  <u>plan</u> <u>on</u> / <u>to</u> 63% M.G.D.

  <u>intend</u> 26% S.

  <u>expect</u> 17% P. X

  <u>figure</u> (<u>on</u>) 16% P. XI

  <u>hope</u> (<u>to</u>) 15% P. XI

  <u>going</u> <u>to</u> 7%

74.4   <u>pick</u> <u>flowers</u>

  <u>pick</u> 92% G.C.-N.

  <u>cut</u> 23% S. P. XIX

  <u>gather</u> 16% P. II, XVIIa

74.5   That's the one you) <u>gave</u> (me

  <u>gave</u> 92% G.C.-N.

  <u>give</u> 13% S.

74.6   He) <u>began</u> (to talk

  <u>began</u> 73% G.C.-N.

74.6 cont.

> started 41% S.
>
> commenced 17% P. V

74.7   He) ran (ashore

> ran 83% G.C.-N.
>
> run 25% S.

74.8   He) came (over to see me

> came 83% G.C.-N.
>
> come 37% M.G.D.

75.1   He) saw (me go in

> saw 89% G.C.-N.
>
> seen 20% S.

75.2   The road was all) torn up

> torn up 72% M.G.D.
>
> tore up 23% S.

75.4   He) did it (last night

> did 83% G.C.-N.
>
> done 23% S.

A SELECTED BIBLIOGRAPHY

The American College Dictionary. New York, 1947.

Atwood, E. Bagby. The Regional Vocabulary of Texas. University of Texas, 1962.

Baugh, Ruth E. The Geographic Regions. (A Syllabus.) Los Angeles, 1953.

Bancroft, H. H. History of California. San Francisco, 1884-1890.

——. History of Nevada, Colorado, and Wyoming. San Francisco, 1890.

Bloomfield, Leonard. Language. New York, 1933.

Bright, William, ed. Studies in Californian Linguistics. UCPL, vol. 34. Berkeley, Calif., 1964.

Buckner, Claudia. "Marble Terminology in California and Nevada: A Vocabulary and Analysis," 1967. Unpublished.

Caughey, John Walton. California, 2nd ed. Englewood Cliffs, N.J., 1953.

Castillo, Carlos, and Otto F. Bond, compilers. The University of Chicago Spanish Dictionary. Chicago, 1948.

Coy, Owen Cochran. The Great Trek. Los Angeles, 1931.

Davis, Alva L. Word Atlas of the Great Lakes Region. (Microfilm) University of Michigan, 1948.

Davis, Sam P., ed. The History of Nevada, vol. II. Reno, 1913.

Durrenberger, Robert W. Patterns on the Land. Woodland Hills, California, 1965.

Emeneau, M. B. "The Dialect of Lunenburg, Nova Scotia," Language 11.2, June, 1935.

Federal Writers' Project, Nevada. Origin of Place Names. Nevada. Reno, 1941.

Gudde, Erwin G. California Place Names. Berkeley, 1960.

Hafen, Leroy R., and Ann W. The Old Spanish Trail, Santa Fe to Los Angeles. Glendale, California, 1954.

——. Journals of the Forty-Niners, Salt Lake to Los Angeles. Glendale, California, 1954.

Hankey, Clyde T. "A Colorado Word Geography," Publication of the American Dialect Society, No. 34, Nov. 1960.

Harder, Kelsie B. "The Vocabulary of Marble Playing," Publication of the American Dialect Society, No. 23, April, 1955, 3-34.

Harris, Benjamin Butler, edited by Richard H. Dillon. The Gila Trail. Norman Oklahoma, 1960.

Kroeber, A. L. Handbook of the Indians of California, Bulletin 78 of the Bureau of American Ethnology. Washington, D.C., 1925.

Kurath, Hans. A Word Geography of the Eastern United States. Ann Arbor, 1949.

Lantis, David W., Rodney Steiner, and Arthur E. Karinen. California: Land of Contrast. Belmont, California, 1963.

Mencken, H. L., edited by Raven I. McDavid, Jr. The American Language. New York, 1963.

Moody, Ralph. The Old Trails West. New York, 1963.

The Oxford English Dictionary. Oxford, 1933.

Reed, Carroll E. "Washington Words," Publication of the American Dialect Society, No. 25, April, 1956, 3-11.

Reed, David W. "Eastern Dialect Words in California," Publication of the American Dialect Society, No. 21, April, 1954, 3-15.

Rolle, Andrew F. California, A History. New York, 1963.

Stewart, George R. The California Trail. New York, 1962.

Thompson, Warren S. Growth and Changes in California's Population. Haynes Foundation, Los Angeles, 1955.

United States Census Office. Ninth Census, 1870, Vol. I, The Statistics of the Population of the United States. Washington, 1872.

――――. Statistics of the Population of the United States at the Tenth Census (1880). Washington, 1883.

――――. Census Reports Vol. I, Twelfth Census of the United States taken in the year 1900. Population, Part I. Washington, 1901.

Wood, Gordon R. "Word Distribution in the Interior South," Publication of the American Dialect Society, No. 35, April, 1961, 1-16.

Zierer, C. M., ed. California and the Southwest. New York, 1956.

INDEX

The decimal number immediately following each entry refers to the category in the General Vocabulary (Appendix) and, for some items, is included for definition purposes only. The letter M preceding a number refers to map number; the letter T refers to table number. Phonetic transcriptions are within brackets.

pret.   preterite
p.p.   past participle
cmpd.   compound.

active   59.5; 59.6, T35
acts like   54.1, M41, T19, T35
adobe(s)   9.8, T25; 10.7, T11, T27, T30, T34
adobe blocks   9.8
(a)dobe bricks   9.8, T11, T25
afraid   59.7
after   28.4
afternoon   3.4, T34
agates   71.6, T10
aggies   71.6, M35, T16, T32
ain't   21.2
ain't I   21.6
a little   69.2
alkali + cmpds.   25.3
all at once   2.6
(all) at one time   2.6, T12
all in   60.5, T35
almond   45.8
almost fell (down)   57.2
alter   32.2, T22
am going   21.1
am I not   21.6
am not   21.2
andirons   6.6, T33

angle-(ing)   65.6, T34
angleworm   49.7, T33
angry   60.3, T34
anti-godlin/goglin   65.6, T34
Appaloosa   30.1, T15, T22, T32, T35
apricot   45.1, T22
aren't I   21.6
Arkies   56.6, T16, T35; 56.8
arroyo   26.2, T27, T30, T34
as far as   35.4
as I/me   36.6
a-singin'   47.8
asphalt   27.2, T35
ate (pret.) 41.8; (p.p.) 42.1
at his stomach   63.2, T33
at home   27.8, T25, T33
at once   2.6, T7
attic   8.3, T34
auto   20.1, T14, T22
automobile   20.1
awakened   72.7
awoke   72.7, T14

(baby) buggy   53.7, T33
baby carriage   53.7, T33

baby lima(s) (beans) 46.6

backhouse 11.2, T33

back log 6.8, T22, T34

back of 8.6

back porch 9.3, T35

back steps 9.3, T11, T34

(bacon) rind 39.5

bag 16.5; 16.6, T34; 23.5

baker('s) bread 37.8

bakery bread 37.8

ball 64.1, T23

bandanna 22.8

barb wire fence 13.5, T35

barbed wire fence 13.5, T23

barley bag 16.7

barley sack 16.7, T6, T10, T22, T35

barn 12.1; 12.7, T6, T25

barnyard 13.2, T22, T33

barranca 25.6 and .7; 26.2 and .3, T27

barrel 15.6

basement 8.8

bastard 54.4, T33

bath towel 15.5

batten 9.6, M41, T19

bawl 32.3; 32.5, T23, T33

bay 25.1, T19, T24, T35

bayos/speckled __ 46.8, M31, T12, T28, T35

beach 26.6

beams 10.8

bear claw 38.1

became ill 60.8, T6, T10, T25, T35

became sick 60.8, T5, T25, T35

because 68.1

bedspread 24.2, T34

been thinking 11.6

began 74.6

behind 8.6

bellow 32.3, T15

belly band 34.5, T23, T34

belly-bust(er) 71.1, T13, T22, T33

belly flop 71.1, T33

billfold 23.6

bit 28.8

bite (to eat) 41.6, T14, T25, T33

bitten 28.8

black diamond (rattler) 50.3

black frost 5.8, T7, M28, T10

blacksnake 16.4, T11, T15, T34

black-top 27.2, T34

blat 32.3, T15

blew 5.5

boar 31.6

board 'n' battens 9.6, M41, T19, T35

bob wire fence 13.5, T34

bog + cmpds. 24.7, T5, T22, T34

boggy mire 24.7, T5, T22

bony 71.6, T32

boogeyman 68.7, T34

boot 56.5, T32

boughten bread 37.8, M34, T15

boulder purie 71.6, T32

boy 56.5, T32

bracero 56.8, T27

bread 37.5, T5, T33

breaking 4.7, T15, T34

breakwater 26.8, T22

breeches 22.5, T5, T22

breezeway 9.5

bring 73.5

broke off (with him) 63.6, T25

bronc 29.8, T28, T34

bronc buster 56.2, T28

bronco 29.8, T27, T30, T34

brook 24.8, T33

brought 21.5

brought up 54.2, T22, T34

brown beans   46.8, T12, T34

buck (v.)   30.4, T34

buck (n.)   31.2, T33

buckaroo   56.2, T15, M44, T23, T28, T35

bucked off (of)   30.3, M31, T12, T22

bucket   14.1

bucket + cmpds.   14.2, T33

bugaboo   68.7, T14, T35

(in) bulk   43.6

bull   29.2

bull calf   29.3

bumbershoot   23.8, T24

bun   38.1, T17

bundle   36.1, T9, T33

bureau   7.7, M43, T22, T34

burial ground(s)   62.2, M31, T12, T22

burlap bag   16.7, T5, T22, T33

burlap sack   16.7, T6, T10, T33

burro   31.1, T27, T30, T34

burro trail   27.3, T27

bushel   36.2, T9, T25

bushels   36.2

butter bean   46.5, T33

butterhorn   38.1, M33, T14

cabinet   11.2, M51, T31

cable car   65.7

calcimine   11.1

cake doughnut   38.2, T34

calf (n.)   29.3; (v.)   29.4, T35

call horses by name   33.5, T6, T34

call horses by whistling   33.5, T34

calling on   63.5, T18, T35

calm down   60.4

calming down   5.6, T14, T34

calve   29.4, T35

came   74.8

came up/come up   3.6, M24, T6, T34

can   16.8

canal   26.3, T34

canopy   9.5, T5, T10

cantaloupe   47.5

canyon   25.6, T34

car   20.1

carne seco   39.7, T27

carried   73.4, T34

casita   11.2, T27

casket   62.3

castrate   32.2

catch-colt   54.4, T18, T33

cate(r)-cornered   65.6

cat's eyes   71.6, T32

cattle barn   12.1

catty-corner(ed)   65.6, T34

caught   73.7

caught a cold   61.1, T25, T34

caught cold   61.1, T34

'cause/cuz   68.1

cayuse   29.8, T31; 30.1, M51, T31

cellar   8.8

cement (road)   27.1, T34, T35

cemetery   62.2

certainly   69.4

chalkies   71.6, T32

changing/changed   4.7, T22, T35

chesterfield   7.4, M37, T17, T35

chesterfield set   7.5, T17

chesterfield suit/suite   7.5

chest of drawers   7.7, T34

chew   43.2

chick   34.2, T33

chicken coop   32.8

chicken house   32.8, T22

Chic Sale(s)   11.2, T25

chiffonier   7.7, T34

chigger/jigger   51.2, T34

chim(b)ley   6.4, T15

chimney   6.4

china (egg)   13.8

chinas/chinies   71.6, T17, T32

chinks   71.6, T32

chinook   5.7, T17, M42, T21, M51, T31

chip beef   39.7, T8

chipmunk   48.7, T33

chipped beef   39.7

cholo   57.1, T11, T27, T30, T35

chonks   71.6, T32

choreman   56.3, M39, T18

chores/(time to) do the chores   33.2, T7, T35

chore time   33.2, T34

Christmas gift!   70.3

chuck hole   27.4

ciénega   24.7, T27

cinch   34.5, T34

cinnamon roll   38.1, M44, T23

city square   65.5

civet/civic/civvy cat   48.6, T15, T34

civic center   65.5

clabber milk   40.6, T33

clabbered (milk)   40.6, T22

clapboards   9.6, T22, T34

cleans (the) house   8.5, T34

cleans (up)   8.5, T34

clear   24.6, T33

clearies   71.6, T32

clearing (up)   4.7, T34

climbed (pret.)   72.1; (p.p.) 72.2

cling peach/clings   44.7, T33

cling-stone (peach)   44.7, T33

close   9.1

closet   7.8

clothes basket   17.1

clothes closet   7.8, T33

clothes hamper   17.1, T11

cloudburst   4.8, T34

clucking   33.6, T33

clum (pret.)   72.1; (p.p.) 72.2

coal bucket   19.4, T33

coal hod   19.4, T9, T33

coal oil   20.5, T33

(coal) scuttle   19.4, M27, T9, T33

coast   26.6, T17

coat(ing) of ice   6.2, T18

cobbler   41.1

cobweb   51.3, 51.4, T34

cock of hay   12.6

coffee cake   38.1, T25

coffin   62.3

coin purse   23.5, T8, T10, T23

colored man/person/people/folks   56.4, T25, T34

come (pret.)   74.8

come again   70.2

come back (again) (soon)   70.2

come boss(ie)   33.3, T23, T33

comfort(er)   24.4, T33

commenced   74.6, T9

commies   71.6, T32

comps   71.6, T32

común   11.2, T27

concrete + cmpds.   27.1, T34, T35

cook (supper)   41.7, T22

coon   56.5, T14, T22, T34

coop   32.8, T8

cork   17.3

corked   60.5, T17, T35

(corn) bin   12.2, M30, T11, T34

corn bread   37.6

corn crib   12.2, T33

corn on the cob   47.2, T34

(corn) silk   47.3, T14

corral   13.2, T27, T30, T34

cottage cheese   40.8, T33

couch   7.4, T34

country hick   56.6, T35

country road 27.3

courting 63.5, T34

cove 25.1, M28, T10, T35

cow barn 12.1; 12.7

cowboy 56.2, T34

cowhand 56.2, T6, T10, T34

cowpuncher 56.2, T6, T34

(cow) shed 12.7

cranberry beans 46.8, M38, T17, T24, T35

crawdad 49.4

crawfish 49.4

crawl 71.8

crayfish 49.4

creek 24.8, T33; 25.1, M36, T17, T33

creep 71.8

crib 12.2, T33

crick 24.8, T34

crocker(ies) 71.6, T32

crystal 71.6, T18

cur 28.6, T22, T34

curdled (milk) 40.6, M33, T14, T33

curtains 7.6, M25, T7, M43, T22, T33

cut (n.) 26.5, T17, T24

cut (v.) 32.2; 36.3; 74.4, T25

cut class/school 64.2, T14, T35

dad 52.8, T34

daddy 52.8, T24, T34

daddy-long-legs 50.6, T32

dairy barn 12.1

damsel fly 50.6, T32

dance 64.1

Danish pastry 38.1, T17

dark 3.7, T25, T35

davenport 7.4, T34

dawn 3.5, T7, T25, T34

daybed 7.4, T14, T35

daylight 3.5, T34

deaf 61.6

deep (dish) (apple) pie 41.1

depot 65.4, T35

desert 25.2, T18

desert canary (bird) 31.1, T32

desert(land) 25.3, T11

devil 68.7

(devil's) darning needle 50.6, T33

devil('s) fly 50.6, T32

devil needle 50.6, T32

devil stinger 50.6, T32

[dʒɛlɪ duᵘts/dʌts] 40.3, M51, T31

diagonal(ly) 65.6, T35

diamond back (rattler) 50.3

diamond (head) 50.3

did 75.4

didn't use to 59.8

died from 62.1, M23, T5, T25

died of 62.1

dime store 70.8, T34

dinner 41.7

dirt road 27.3

dish cloth 15.2; 15.3, T34

dish rag 15.2

dish towel 15.3, T34

ditch 26.3

ditched 64.2, T11, T34

divan 7.4, T25, T34

dived 71.4

dobabes/dobabies 71.6, T15, T32

dobe 9.8, T11, T25; 10.7, T11, T28, T34

dobies 71.6, T32

dock 26.7

does the (house) cleaning 8.5, T17, T24

does the housework 8.5, T17, M45, T24, T35

doesn't 11.5

dogie   29.5, T25, T34

dog irons   6.6, T33

done   11.4; (pret.) 75.4

donkey   31.1, M26, T8, T34

don't   11.5

doubletree   17.7, T34

doughnut   38.2, T33; 38.3

dove   71.4

doughboys   71.6, T32

doughie   71.6, T32

down in the dobe   56.7, T32

downpour   4.8, M46, T25, T34

dragon fly   50.6, T33

drank (pret.)   42.5; (p.p.) 42.6

dreamed   72.6

dreamt   72.6

[drɛk]   8.2, M51, T31

dremp   72.6

dresser   7.7, T34

dressing table   7.7, T11, T25, T35

dried beef   39.7, T6, T10

drive   73.1, T11, T35

driven   10.2

drought   5.4, T34

drouth   5.4, T34

drove (pret.)   10.1; (p.p.) 10.2, T6

drownded   71.5

drowned   71.5

drunk (pret.)   42.5; (p.p.) 42.6

dry spell   5.4, T34

dry year   5.4, T11, T35

Dutch oven   14.6, M30, T11

dying (down)   5.6, T34

ear sewer   50.6, M38, T17, T32,
    T34

ears of corn   47.2, T15, T22, T35

earthworm   49.7, T33

east   38.7, T22

eat   (p.p.) 42.1

eaten   42.1

eaves   10.4, T34

eaves troughs   10.4, T22, T33

education   64.3

either you or I/me   57.7

electric(al) storm   5.1, T34

elementary school   64.4, T25

embarcadero   26.7, T27

emery wheel   19.7, T6, T10, T35

et   (p.p.) 42.1

evening   3.4, T11, T34

excited   60.3, T12, T35

exhausted   60.5, M46, T25, T35

expect   74.3, T14

face cloth   15.4, T14, T25

face rag   15.4, T14

fairly 69.2, T17

family   53.2, T14, T25, T35; 53.3,
    T14, T22, T35

['fæŋkjuᵗᵗˌmaᵗᵗnz]   27.4, T32

farm   13.3

farm hand   56.3

farmer   56.6, T25, T35

fartherest   35.4

farthest   35.4, T25

fascinator   22.8

[faʃnaks]   38.2, M51, T31

father   52.8, T35

faucet   16.1, T33; 16.2, T35; 16.3,
    T35

feed bag   34.7, T34

feed barn   12.1

feeding time   33.2, T23, T34

['fɛɚɪbiʃ]   50.6, M51, T31

fifteen cent store   70.8, T12, T35

fifteen (minutes) to eleven   4.4,
    T12, T17, T35

figure (on)   74.3, T15

[fɪⁱlɪⁱə]   40.8, M51, T31

fire dogs 6.6, T33
firefly 50.5, T33
fire irons 6.6, T35
first grade 64.5
fish(ing) worm 49.7, T15, T24, T33
fit 22.6
fitted 22.6
five and dime (store) 70.8, T35
five and ten 70.8, T25, T34
five and ten cent store 70.8, T35
fix (supper) 41.7, T25
flapjacks 38.4, M26, T8, T34
flat iron 19.8
flat(lands) 25.2, T33
flicker 48.5, T15, T25
flipper (crutch) 19.1, M42, T21,
    T32, T35
flying mosquito 50.6, T32
folks 53.2, T34; 53.3, T15, T34
for 28.4, T22
for you 73.8
frame of mind 74.1, T18
frau 52.6, M51, T31
free-stone(peach) 44.8, T33
freeze 5.8, T25
fresh corn 47.2, T15, T22, T35
frightened 59.7
frijoles 46.8, T27, T34
Frisco 67.7
frog 49.5, T34
front porch 9.2, T34
front room 6.3, T10, T33
frost 5.8
frosting 41.3
froze 6.1
froze over 6.1
fruit tramp 56.8, T15
frying pan 14.5, T33
furniture 7.5, T6
furniture set 7.5

furtherest 35.4
furthest 35.4

gallinipper 50.6, T32
galoshes 24.1
gap 26.5, T14, T25
garbage can 14.4, T34
garbage pail 14.4, T35
garden 11.8, T5; 43.3, T9, T34
garden worm 49.7, T16, T35
garret 8.3, T17, T34
gather 36.4; 74.4, T6, T22
gave 74.5
gave him the gate/the air, etc.
    63.6
get 73.5
get (supper) 41.7
get up 33.6, T33
ghosts 68.8, T34
giddy up 33.6, T33
gilt 31.5, T12
give (pret.) 74.5
give you a lift 73.1, T6, T10, T22,
    T35
give you a ride (home) 73.1, T8,
    T10, T35
glass 7.7, T6, T10
glass egg 13.8
glassies 71.6, T10, T32
(glass) stopper 17.4
glazies 71.6, T32
glowworm 50.5, T14, T25, T35
gnat hawk 50.6, T32
go and get 73.5
God! 68.6
go get 73.5, M45, T24
going steady (with) 63.5, T34
going to 74.3
going together 63.5, T19, T35
going with 63.5, T25, T34

good   35.1

good God!   68.6, T17

good humor   74.1

good mood   74.1

good morning   3.3

good spirits   74.1, T22

goose flesh   60.7

goose pimples   60.7

gopher   48.7, M30, T11, T35

gorge   25.6; 25.7, T34

gosling drownder   4.8, T32

got sick   60.8, T34

grade school   64.4

grammar school   64.4

granary   12.3, T24

grandfather   53.4, T34

grandma   53.5, T34

grandmother   53.5, T34

grandpa   53.4, T34

graveyard   62.2

greaser   57.1, T22, T34

green beans   46.7, M25, T7, T33

green corn   47.2, T15, T22, T34

green onion   46.3

griddle cakes   38.4, T15; M45, T24;
   T33

grindstone   19.7, T34

grossmutter   53.5, M51, T31

grosspapa   53.4, M51, T31

ground squirrel   48.7, T7, T33

grown (up)   54.3

gulch   25.6; 25.8, T34

gully   25.6; 26.1, T34

gums (pron.)   58.5, M42, T21

gunny sack   16.7, T33

gutters   10.4, T33

half (a) load   18.1, T5, T35

half past seven   4.3

handbag   23.5

handirons   6.6, T33

handkerchief   22.8, T12

hard of hearing   61.6

harmonica   19.2, T34

harrow   18.2, T34

hauling   17.8, T33

haunches   59.1

have a calf   29.4, T35

have been thinking   11.6

haybarn   12.1

haycock   12.6, T33

hayloft   12.4, T33

(hay)mow   12.4, T33

hayseed   56.6, T34

(hay)shock   12.6, T33

haystack   12.5, T33; 12.6, T5, T24,
   T34

head cheese   40.3, T34

hearth   6.5

heave   62.8, T6; 63.1, T25

heavy frost   5.8, M26, T8, T10, T25

heavy rain   4.8, T7, T35

heifer (calf)   29.3

help you home   73.1, T6, T10, T35

henhouse   32.8

herdsman   56.2, T15, T35

here/there are your clothes   21.4

here boss(ie)   33.3, T25, T35

here's/there's your clothes   21.4

hick   56.6, T34

high spirits   74.1, T22

hillbilly   56.6, T25, T34

hired man   56.3, T25

hitched (up)   63.7, T22

hm?   44.3

[hm?m/?m?m]   69.7, T6

[hɪn^{t}ʃtən]   27.7, M51, T31

hoedown   64.1, T18

hog   31.5

hogpen   12.8, T22, T33

hole 27.4

hombre 57.1, T27

home 27.8, T34

home garden 43.3, T15, T35

hominy (grits) 43.4

hoofs 30.6

hooves 30.6, T25

hope (to) 74.3, T15

hornet 50.8

horned toad 49.6, T10, T34

horn toad 49.6, T34

horny toad 49.6, T11, T34

horse 18.4, T7, T24, T33

horse barn 12.1

horseshoes 30.7; 30.8, T34

hot (around/under the collar) 60.3,
   T18, T35

hot cakes 38.4, T33

how are you? 69.8

how (are) you feeling? 69.8

how do you do? 70.1

hoya 25.5, T27

huh? 44.3

huh-uh/uh-uh 69.7, T25

hull (n.) 45.4, T34; (v.) 46.4, T33

husband 52.5

husk 45.4, T33; 47.1, T33

husky 59.2

hydrant 16.3, T22, T34

icing 41.3

I'll be 63.3

illegitimate (child) 54.4, T11, T25,
   T33

imies 71.6, T32

Indian shooter 19.1, T32

indolent 60.6, M32, T13, T35

inlet 25.1, T10, T24, T35

intend 74.3

iron 19.8

irrigation ditch 26.3, T34

is (just) like 54.1, T19, T35

it wasn't I 21.7

it wasn't me 21.7

[(ɪ)jæl] 69.5, T6

jackass 31.1, T34

jag 18.1, T33

jalopy 20.1, T16

jam 43.7, T8, T10

jaundice 62.7

jeans 22.5, M34, T15

jelly 43.7

jerky 39.7

Jew's harp 19.3

jilted 63.6

joists 10.8, T25

juice harp 19.3, T9, T22

junk 8.2, T34

junk room 8.4, T14, T33

keep calm 60.4

kerosene 20.5, T33

kettle 14.6

kindling 7.1, T33

kind of 69.2

kiss-me-mams 27.4, T32

kitty-corner(ed) 65.6, T35

kneeled 72.3

knelt 72.3

knit 23.2

knitted 23.2

knitting needle 50.6, T32

knock 36.4

knosch 41.6, M51, T31

Kress's 70.8

L. A. 67.5

lag(ging) line 71.7, T25

laid 72.5

lanai   9.4, 9.5, M51, T31
land turtle   50.2
langosta   49.4, T27
lariat   34.8, M27, T9, T28, T34
lasso   34.8, T28, T34
lass(o) rope   34.8, T35
latigo   34.5, T27
laundry   8.7
lawn   11.8, T18, T22
lay   72.5
lay down   72.4
lazy   60.6, T34
lead horse   34.6, T25, T33
lean-to   10.6, T34
leftover(s)/food   43.1, M26, T8, T10
leppy   29.5, T11, T15, T23, T35
letter carrier   56.1, T17
letting up   5.6, T25, T34
lie down   72.4
light bread   37.5, T15, T23, T33
light frost   5.8, T8, T10
lightning bug   50.5, T33
lima bean   46.5, T33; 46.6
limas   46.6
lines   34.3
(a) little way(s)   35.2
lively   59.5, T25; 59.6, T25, T35
liver sausage   40.4
liverwurst   40.4
livestock barn   12.1
living room   6.3, T33
lobster   49.4, .M38, T17
loft   12.4
log   6.8, T35
(a) long way(s)   35.3
look at this/that   57.5, T6, T10
look here   57.5
looking glass   7.7, T6, T10
looks like   54.1, T34
Los Angeles (pron.)   67.5

lot   11.8, T14
lounge   7.4, T34
loveseat   7.4, T14, T35
lugged   73.4, T22, T34
lunch box   14.3, T34
lunch bucket   14.3, T34
lunch pail   14.3, M46, T25, T34

ma   53.1, T11, T25, T34
macadam(ized) (road)   27.2, T24,
    T35
machine   20.1, T14
mad   60.3, T34
madre   53.1, T27
mail carrier   56.1, T22
mailman   56.1
make (some) coffee   42.2
mama   53.1, T34
mama grande   53.5, M51, T31
mantel   6.7, T33
mantelpiece   6.7, T33
(maple) grove   51.7, T33
(maple) orchard   51.7, T8, T10,
    T33
maple (tree)   51.6, T34
marbles   71.6
married   63.7
marsh   24.7
maverick   29.5, T34
may be able to   48.4
meadow(s)/(land)   25.4, T23, T34;
    25.5, T22
megs   71.6, T32
members   56.5, T32
Merry Christmas   70.3
mesa   25.2, T25, T27, T30, T34
Mesican   57.1, T32
Mexican   57.1, T34
(Mexican) nationals   57.1, T15, T35
m-hm   69.5

mibs (game of mibs) 71.6, T32

midwife 53.8, T33

might (be able to) 48.4

migrant(s) (worker) 56.8, T6

migratory worker 56.8

migs (-ies) 71.6, T19, T32

milk barn 12.1

miller 50.3, T14

minnow 50.1, T34

miser(ly) 59.3, T34, T35

mom 53.1, T34

mongrel 28.6, T34

moo 32.4, T33

moonies 71.6, T32

morral 34.7, T27

mosquito catcher 50.6, T32

mosquito hawk 50.6, T15, T32, T33

mossies 71.6, T32

moth 50.4

mother 53.1, T34

mountain canary 31.1, T32

mouth organ 19.2, T34

mouth stitcher 50.6, T32

mud dauber 50.7, T15, T25, T34

muscular 59.2, T12

mushmelon 47.5

muskmelon 47.5

mustang 29.8, T6, T28

my God! 68.6

nana 53.5, T27

near horse 34.6, T22, T33

nearly fell (down) 57.2, T7, T23

needle bug 50.6, T32

needle fly 50.6, T32

negro 56.4, T34

neigh 32.6, M27, T9, T25, T34

neither you nor/or I 57.8

nest(ing) egg 13.8

never used to 59.8

never was 59.8

nicker 32.6, T22, T33

nigger 56.5, T34

nigger shooter 19.1, T32

nigh horse 34.6, T12, T33

night crawler 49.8

no 69.7

no-can-see 51.2, T32

no-good colored person 56.5, T32

no-see-'em 51.2, T32

none 35.5

nono 53.4, M51, T31

nope 69.7, T14

nose bag 34.7, T34

not a one 35.5

not any 35.5

notch 26.5

notion store 70.8, T18, T24, T35

novelty store 70.8, T18, T22, T35

nut 20.6

obstinate 60.2, T22

ocean 26.6

off horse 34.6, T5, T34

off (of) 30.3

oil(ed) road 27.2, T8, T35

Okies 56.6, M35, T16, T22, T35;
     56.8

old wreck 20.1

opera house 65.3, T6, M28, T10,
     T22

ornery/onery 60.2, T15

orphan 29.5, T23, T34

ought not/oughtn't 48.2

out-house 11.2, T33

(out) in the country 56.7

(out) in the sticks 56.7, T34

out in the tules/tule bushes 56.7,
     T32, T34

overalls 22.5, T15

overshoes   24.1

over there   44.2, T34

over yonder   44.2, T34

pa   52.8, T11, T24, T34

pachuco/pachuke   57.1, T28

packed   73.4, T8, T34

paddy   56.6, T32

pail   14.2, T33

paint (v.)   11.1;   (n.)   30.1, T24,
    T34

paisano   57.1, T27

pallet   24.5, T15, T33

pancakes   38.4, T33

pants   22.5

papa   52.8, T34

papa grande   53.4, M51, T31

paper bag   16.5, T33

paper route (pron.)   55.7, T22

paper sack   16.5, T33

parasol   23.8, T15

pardner   54.8

pardon (me)?   44.3

parents   53.2, T34

park   65.5

parking   27.6, T34

parkway   27.6, T7, M28, T10, T34

parlor   6.3, M33, T14, T35

partner   54.8

pass   26.5

patio   9.4, T27, T30

paved road   27.1, T34

peace and order   66.1

peanut   45.2, T35

(peanut) shell   45.5

peckerwood   56.6, T32

peeved   60.3, T12, T35

peewees   71.6, T32

peon   57.1, T27, T30

peppy/full of pep   59.5

perspired   61.7, T11, T34

pests   48.8, T35

pick   36.3; 36.4; 74.4

picket fence   13.4, T33

piece(meal)(ing)   41.6, T33

pier   26.7

pig   31.5

pig barn   12.1

(pig) pen   12.8, T33

pig! pig!   33.8, T33

(pig) sty   12.8, T23, T33

pillowcase   24.3, T34

(pillow)slip   24.3, T34

pine nut/pie nut   45.8, T18, M45,
    T24

pink beans   46.8, T35

pinto   30.1, T28, T34

pinto beans   46.8, T34

pit   44.5, T34; 44.6, T34

plain   25.2, T6, T22, T34

plains   25.4, T8, T34

plane/oriental plane   51.8, T17,
    T35

plan on/to   74.3

plateau   25.2, T34

played hookey   64.2, T33

played/was truant   64.2, T14, T22,
    T33

playhouse   65.3, M31, T12, T22

plaza   65.5, T27, T30

pleased to meet you   70.1

pocketbook   23.5

pogalip   5.3, M51, T31

poganip   5.7, T31

poganip frost   5.8, M51, T31

poison   52.4

poisonous   52.4

pole cat   48.6, T33

polenta   37.6, T31; 40.5, M51, T31

pooped (out)   60.5, T34

pop 42.7, T34

porch 9.2, T33; 9.3, T35

pork 39.4, T33

['pɔʌʃəˌʃɛʌ] 9.5, M51, T31

['poʌpaʃɛʌ] 9.2, M51, T31

portable wardrobe 8.1, T35

porte cochere 9.2, T31; 9.5, T31, M51

postman 56.1

pot 14.6, T23

potato yeast 38.8, M34, T15

potrero 25.2; 25.5; 26.2, T27

potsies 71.6, T32

potteries 71.6, T21, T32

potters 71.6, T32

potters field 62.2, T16

pounds 38.6

pour-down 4.8, T17, T32, T34

powerful 59.2, T12, T22

prairie 25.2, T24

prairie (land) 25.4, T34

praline 45.7

prawn(s) 49.1

prepare (supper) 41.7, T25

preserves 43.7, T8, T10

pretty 69.2, T6

primary (school)/(grades) 64.4, T22

primary (grade)/(class)/(department) 64.5, T17

privy 11.2, T33

prongs 49.1, T14

public school 64.4, M32, T13

public square 65.5

puke 63.1

pupil 55.6

puries 71.6, T14, T32

purse 23.5

quarter of eleven 4.4, T33

quarter to eleven 4.4, T33

quilt 24.4, T33, T34

rafters 10.8

railroad station 65.4, T34

(rain) storm 4.8, T14, T34

raised 54.2, T34

raised doughnut 38.3, T33

ram 31.2, T33

ran 74.7

ranch 13.3

rancher 56.6, T15, T35

ranchero 56.2, T27

ranch hand 56.2; 56.3

rancid 40.1

rather 69.2

rattler 50.3

rattlesnake 50.3

ravine 25.7, T34

realies 71.6, T32

rear (up) 30.4, T35

reared 54.2, T22, T34

reata 34.8, T23, T27, T30, T34

receipt 38.5, T8, T22

reception 63.8, T18, T35

rechauffé 43.1, M51, T31

recipe 38.5

reins 34.3

relations 53.3, T34

relatives 53.3, T34

remada 9.2, 9.5, T27

resembles 54.1, T34

ridden 30.2

(right) there 44.2

rinch/rench 15.1, T7, T10, T22, T34

rincon 25.5, T27

rinse 15.1, T34

river 24.8, T33

roasting ears 47.2, T15, T33

rock 27.7

rock fence   13.7, T33
rock wall   13.7, T7, T33
rocky mountain canary   31.1, T32
rode   30.2
rodent   48.8, T22, T35
rodeo (pron.)   29.9, M50, T27, T28, T30
rose   3.6, T34
roustabout   56.3, T18
route (of a trip) (pron.)   55.7, T25
rubbers   24.1
rubbish   8.2, T11, T35
run (pret.)   74.7
rustic   9.6, M39, T18, T35
rut   27.4

sack   16.5; 16.6, T35
sacks   36.2
sad iron   19.8
salt pork   39.4, T33
Sambo   56.5, T32
San Berdoo   67.5
San Bernardino   67.5
San Fran   67.7, T18
San Francisco   67.7
sanky   26.3, M41, T19, T28, T35
Santa Ana   5.7, M40, M41, T19, T27
sapsucker   48.5, T12
sat   42.8
Satan   68.7, T34
Saturday   3.2
sauce   41.2, T34
saw   75.1
saw-buck   18.5, T33
saw-horse   18.4, T33; 18.5, T34
scared   59.7
scarf   22.8
scholar   55.6, T22
school boy/girl   55.6, T6, T22
scrapple   40.5, T22, T33

scythestone   19.6, T12, T34
seawall   26.8, T14
second crop   35.8, T9, T33
second cutting   35.8, T33
seed   44.5, T10, T34; 44.6, M25, T7, T10, T34
seen (pret.)   75.1
seesaw   18.8, T33
see you home   73.1, T11, T24, T34
set (pret.)   42.8
set in his ways   60.2, T6
set (of furniture)   7.5
settee   7.4, T34
setting hen   32.7
seven-thirty   4.3
sewing bug   50.6, T32
sewing needle   50.6, T32
S.F.   67.7, T6, T10, T22
['ʃaₗbᵊ/ɪs]   3.2, M51, T31
shades   7.6
shafts   17.5, T34
shakes   9.7
shall   63.3; 63.4
shavs   17.5, T34
sheaf   36.1, T22, T34
shed   10.5, T34; 10.6, T11, T34
sheep barn   12.1
shell (v.)   46.4, T33
shindig   64.1, T15, T22
shiner   50.1, M38, T17, T22, T34
shiplap   9.6, M23, T5, T35
shivaree   63.8, T33
shoat   31.5, T15, T22
shock (of hay)   12.6, T33; (of wheat)   36.1, T15, T34
shoes   30.7, T7, M44, T23
shooters   71.6, T15, T32
short distance   35.2, T22
short ways   35.2, T9, T25
shouldn't   48.2

show house 65.3, T12

shrank 23.3

shrimp(s) 49.1

shrunk 23.3; 23.4

shut 9.1

shy (v.) 30.5

side (of bacon) 39.6, M43, T22, T34

side meat 39.4, T33

side pork 39.4, T33

side road 27.3, T25

sidewinder 50.3

siding 9.6, T35

['sɪlˌsə] 40.3, M51, T31

singletree 17.6, T33; 17.7, T5, T35

sire 29.2, T15, T25

sit (pret.) 42.8

sitting room 6.3, T7, T10, T33

skeeter hawk 50.6, T32

skillet 14.5, T33

skim ice 6.2

skim (of ice) 6.2

skin 39.5, T15

skunk 48.6, T33

slab 39.6, T34

slacks 22.5

sled 18.3, T24, T33

slick 27.5

slingshot 19.1, T34

slippery 27.5

slop bucket 14.4, M24, T6, T10, T15, T33

slough 24.7, T22, T34; 24.8, T18, T35

sloughed school 64.2, M42, T21, T25, T35

small load 18.1, M32, T13

smearcase 40.8, T22, T33

snack 41.6, T33

snail 38.1, T22

snake doctor 50.6, T12, T32, T33

snake feeder 50.6, T15, T32, T33

so boss(ie) 33.4, T33

soda 42.7, T14, T24, T35

soda pop 42.7, T24, T34

sofa 7.4, T34

soft drink 42.7, T34

sour(ed/ing) 40.7, T34

sourdough 38.8, M24, T6, T10

sour milk 40.6, T34

sow 31.5, T9, T10

sow belly 39.4, T33

sparking 63.5, T15, T34

spay 32.2

spicket 16.2, T33

spider 14.5

spiderweb 51.3, T34

spider's web 51.4, T34

spigot 16.2, T33

['spɪkəz] 57.1, T32

spoiled 40.1

spoilt 40.1

somersault 71.2

sponge 15.2, T19

spook(s) 56.5, T32, T34; 68.8

spread 24.2, T34

spry 59.6, T34

stack (of hay) 12.5; 12.6, T5, T24

stallion 29.7, T34

stamp 72.8

start (supper) 41.7, T14, T22

started 74.6

start(er) (of) yeast 38.8, T15

station 65.4, T34

stayed 72.5

steelies 71.6, T15, T32

step(s) 9.3, T11

stinger 50.6, T32

stingy 59.3, T35

stock barn 12.1

stomp 72.8
stone 44.5, T34; 44.6, T34
stone boat 18.3, T33
stone fence 13.7, T33
stone wall 13.7, T23, T33
stonies 71.6, T32
stopping 5.6, M35, T16, T35
storage barn 12.1
storage room 8.4, T5, T35
store bread 37.8, T22
store room 8.4, T33
stream 24.8, T35
street car 65.7
string beans 46.7, T33
strong 59.2
stubborn 60.2
stud(horse) 29.7, T34
student 55.6
['sʊ‡gən] 24.4, T32
sugar maple 51.6, T33
suite (of rooms) 7.5, M23, T5
suite of furniture 7.5
sundown 3.7, T34
sunfish 30.4, T15, T34
sunrise 3.5, T34
sunset 3.7, T25, T34
sun-up 3.5, T10, T34
supper 41.7
sure 69.4
suwee! 33.8, T34
swam 71.3
swamp 24.7
sweat 61.7, T34
sweated 61.7, T34
sweet corn 47.2, T33
sweet roll 38.1
swill barrel/bucket/pail 14.4, T15, T33, T35
swum 71.3
sycamore 51.8, T33

tainted 40.1
taken 61.4
takes after 54.1, T34
take you home 73.1, T33
tap 16.2, T23, T34
tar/tarred road 27.2, M36, T17, T35
tarantula hawk 50.6, T32; 50.7, T32
[tərɔlɚ/taro‡lɚ] 71.6, T32
tassel 47.3
tata 53.4, T27
taught 74.2
taw(s) 71.6, T5, T32
tawl 71.6, T32
taw(line) 71.7
tea kettle 14.6
tea towel 15.3, T34
teeter 18.8, T33
teeterboard 18.8, T22, T33
teeter-totter 18.8, T33
ten-forty-five 4.4, T35
thank-you-mams 27.4, T32
theater 65.3
the city 67.7, M39, T18, T24
them boys 44.1
(thin) coat(ing) of ice 6.2, T14
those boys 44.1
thrashed (is/are) 36.5
threw 27.7
threw him over 63.6
throw up 62.8, 63.1
thunder and lightning (storm) 5.1, T14, T25, T35
   (a thunder and lightning/a lightning and thunder 5.1, M36, T17, T35)
thunderstorm 5.1, T34
tick 51.2, T14
tidies (up) 8.5, T5, T10, T35
tied (up)/tied the knot 63.7, T18

tight 59.3, T34

tightwad 59.3, T25, T34

timber rattler 50.3, M39, T18

tin 16.8

tin can 16.8

tint 11.1, T14, T22

tired (out) 60.5, T35

toad 49.5, T34

toad shooter 19.1, T32

toadstool 47.6

toe line/mark 71.7

to his stomach 63.2, T33

toilet 11.2, M46, T25, T33

tommy hawk 50.6, T32

tommy tailor 50.6, T32

Tonopah canary 31.1, T32

took 61.5

took (a) cold 61.1, T14, T34

took sick/ill 60.8, M25, T7, T25, T34

toolhouse 10.5, T34

toolshed 10.5, T34

tore up (p.p.) 75.2

torn up 75.2

toro 29.2, T27

tortilla 37.7, T27

tortoise 50.2

toward 28.3

towards 28.3, T9

towel 15.5

transient worker/laborer 56.8

trash 8.2, T35

trolley (car) 65.7

trousers 22.5

tule fog 5.2, T17

tule(s)(-land)/(-swamp) 24.7, T18

tule route 56.7, T32

tumble(sault) 71.2, M36, T17

turned him down 63.6

turn(ed/ing) sour 40.7, T35

turtle 50.2

tusk(s) 31.8

uh-huh 69.5

umbrella 23.8

valley 25.5, T35

vaquero 56.2, T24, T27, T30, T34

variety (store) 70.8, T22, T34

varmint 48.8, T34

vase 14.7

vecino 57.1, T27

vegetable garden 43.3, T34

veranda 9.2, T33

vomit 62.8; 63.1, T17

wallet 23.6

(walnut) shell 45.3, T34

want off 65.8, T33

want to get off 65.8, T33

wardrobe 7.8, M30, T11, T22; 8.1, T34

warmed over/up 43.1

wash 14.8, T34

wash/dry wash 26.1

wash cloth 15.4

washing 8.7

washing and ironing 8.7

Washington 67.1

wash rag 15.4

wasn't 59.8

wasp 50.7, T35

was taken sick/ill 60.8, T22, T34

wasteland 25.3, T25

water closet 11.2, M33, T14, T33

web 51.3, T11, T35; 51.4, T11, T35

wed(ded) 63.7, M32, T13, T22

well 35.1

we'll be 63.4

wetback   57.1, T34

wharf   26.7, T22

what   37.3

what/what-all   37.4

what?   44.3

what's that?   44.3

wheelbarrel   19.5, T18

wheelbarrow   19.5

wheel horse/wheeler   34.6, T15, T25,
   T33

whetstone   19.6, T33

whinny   32.6, T9, T33

whip   16.4

whiskers   58.3, T15

white bread   37.5, T33

white frost   5.8, T7, T10

whities   71.6, T32

who/who-all   37.2

who(m)   44.4

whoa   33.7

whose   37.3

widow   52.7

wife   52.6

wild (horse)   29.8, M44, T23, T34

will   63.3; 63.4

(window) blinds   7.6, T33

window shades   7.6, T33

wishbone   33.1, T33

woke up   72.7

wood(en) bucket   14.1, T6, T33

wooden pail   14.1, T33

woodpecker   48.5

woodshed   10.5, T34; 10.6, T6, T34

wood tick   51.2, T17, T35

Woolworth's   70.8, T22, T35

worm   49.7, T34

worn out   60.5, T34

yard   11.8

yeah   69.5

yeast   38.7

yelk   39.2

yellow hammer   48.5, T15, T22

yellow jacket   50.7, T35; 50.8;
   51.1

yellow janders/jaunders   62.7, T17

yellow jaundice   62.7

yes   69.5

yes, sir/ma'am   69.6

yolk   39.2

you/you-all   36.8, T33

yours   36.7

your(s)   37.1

yulk   39.2